Bob-The Jew

© Alan Zoltie 2024. All Rights Reserved.
Alan Zoltie Publishing inc.
ISBN: 978-1-7374122-6-7

For Maggie Mae, our newest addition.
For Bob
For Dave
For Madge
For Arkush
For Dan
For Joan
For Holly
And lastly for Julie

Whether you all read this or not, you all know who you are and have incredible patience and wonderful souls which will one day be set free.

At no time in my writing career have I ever used Ai. At no point do I intend to use Ai. I am a firm believer that Ai can be of assistance to mankind in all sorts of wonderful applications, but for me as a writer, and to all my fellow writers out there, Ai is nothing but an inconvenience and an unfortunate addition for those who cannot write genuine, intelligent and innovative copy, confusing readers who spend good money on purchasing, what they hope, is original material from the minds of their favorite authors.

All work is © Alan Zoltie, and alanzoltie.com, Alan Zoltie Publishing Inc 2024.
Art and art files provided by anninwonderland

Foreword

In recent years, the homeless crisis has reached unprecedented levels, making it a pressing issue that confronts us daily. With the problem prominently featured in the news and visible in our communities, the time has come for us to collectively address this issue through the power vested in each and every one of us. The solution lies within our hands, and more importantly, within our hearts and wallets.

My dear friend Alan Zoltie, whom I have known for many years, is a beacon of hope and action in this realm. Alan's charitable work spans various causes, from addressing the needs of children with special needs to aiding the homeless and supporting numerous other charitable endeavors. His viewpoint and solutions to the problem of homelessness are not only highly valuable but also actionable.

There is an old expression that no wisdom compares to that of someone who has experienced the problem firsthand. Alan has lived and experienced being unhoused by choice, immersing himself in the life of the homeless to gain firsthand knowledge about the crisis. He has witnessed and endured the daily suffering, the challenge of finding a bathroom, securing a safe place to survive the night, and obtaining food. His profound experiences are captured in his book Cardboard City, providing invaluable insights into the plight of the homeless.

The term we often use for helping someone is "charity." In Hebrew, it is called "Tzedaka," which translates not to charity but to "righteousness," meaning it is the right thing to do. It is a matter of justice, not just a feeling of generosity.

The Talmud, (the primary source of Jewish law), records a debate about the need to help the poor. The question arises: if G-d made individuals poor, wouldn't helping them be against G-d's will? The answer given is that G-d created the world in such a way that people need one another; we cannot exist without each other. By helping the poor, you fulfill your obligation and role in this interconnected world. A parable in the Talmud tells of a king who banished his son from his palace without food or money as a punishment. A kind person helped the young prince, and the king rewarded the benefactor for ultimately helping his son. The people on the street are G-d's children; they are someone's child, deserving of our care and attention.

My father once shared an ancient teaching that is difficult to understand but profoundly important. If you see a poor person asking for help and they appear healthy, do not judge or question why they don't just get a job. Do you also wish for them to lose their health? Our job is not to judge; just as we do not want others to judge our shortcomings, we should not judge others. Give them the benefit of the doubt. When you help others, you benefit yourself as much, if not more, than the person receiving your aid.

In this book, we explore the depths of the homeless crisis through Alan's lived experiences and insightful solutions. It is a call to action, urging us to embrace Tzedaka—not out of charity but out of righteousness. Let us recognize that the solution is within our reach, and together, we can make a meaningful difference. By helping others, we fulfill our moral duty and strengthen the fabric of our shared humanity.

Rabbi Aaron Cunin

Part 1

Bob-The Jew

Snot from his nose ran slowly, like a meandering river, onto his thick dirty grey mustache, and then onwards, over his lips, towards his 9-inch-long filthy multicolored and matted beard, a beard that looked like an unkept farm hedge in dire need of a good trim. It settled, eventually, between large clumps of grass, small leaves, and even more dirt, situated below his fat belly, as it dripped, unattended and out of control, and then Bob, took his left hand and ran his disgustingly smelly dark-stained fingers through this barbed wire mess to stop the flow.

As he sat on the 'Osborn' bench, a name he'd given his weekend retreat, (Bob lived Monday to Friday in another, more expensive part of town), his new sunglasses, which had obviously been collected from one of his 'trash can' excursions, sparkled brightly in the afternoon sun, their brown/beige frames, laced with glitter, or was it wear and tear, looking quite out of place on his weather-beaten face. Bob's spare clothes had been discarded on the grassy lawn which lay adjacent to the Osborn bench, a bench named after one of Dana Point's lost heroes, and his sleeping bag, or sheet, covered what remained of the seat where the rest of this Saturday would be spent, and probably every other Saturday, until Bob, who looked like he was pushing 75 or maybe more, passed away, unnoticed, unloved and certainly unwanted, by any other human being on this earth.

And while the afternoon sun shone brightly and the local birds sang joyfully, the ocean on the other side of the hill moved rhythmically in and out to the beat of repetitious tide levels, all of humanity passed by Bob, avoiding his gaze, his philosophical rants, and above all, his stench, his miserable street infused stench, avoiding eye to eye contact, and giving him as wide a berth as was possible on such a small pathway without giving a single thought or a single ounce of sympathy to this man, who, let's face it, was just another homeless human being who might jump up at any moment and while facing them head on, ask them to assist financially with his God-forsaken plight or just to stop and have a civil conversation for a few minutes to break up the monotony of his day which presumably was always the same, so repetitive, so disgusting and so irrevocably mundane. Their guilt, hidden inside hearts that had become all to accustomed to situations like Bob's and the millions of others who shared Bob's unfortunate circumstance, hardened by an acceptance of 'this is just the way it is and the way it's going to be' and complimented by the beliefs of most of these passers by that 'these people' were the 'scum' of the earth and that there was nothing to be done except pass on by, ignore them and hope that someone else took up their irrevocable plight.

But Bob was not like the others, and the others were not like Bob.

Homelessness, so prevalent, so unwelcoming, and today, so common, no matter where you live and what you care to believe, this pandemic of human suffering, some self-inflicted, but mostly just unwanted, typified by people like Bob, all with stories, all with excuses, all with reasons on how and why their luck ran out and then how they got kicked out of society, a society which just marched on unattended, while willing these vagrants out of their sight, even though they can never magically disappear, hoping that someone else will take care of the Bobs of this world. But Bob was going nowhere, and with that in mind, even though he occupied prime real estate on a picturesque walking trail in Dana Point California, on this particular Saturday, I was never going to pass without asking Bob how he was doing. It was, as I had learned at an early age, a 'mitzvah', to be compassionate, and compassionate I would be.

Bob and I had taken up conversation previously, and quite often I'd passed him by asking him how life on the streets was treating him. On some occasions, Bob had been aloof, and on other's he'd waxed lyrical about politics, although I was certain he was directing his knowledge and anger towards the sky and not to me, leaving me to question his sanity, let alone his inability to recognize that all I wanted to do was offer assistance to his day and try to make his miserable life just a little bit better. He would often sit holding his cell phone, a phone that I later discovered did not work, holding conversations with no one in particular, but everyone he could remember. Bearing in mind that every homeless person can receive a fully functional cell phone free of charge, through a program set up by previous government administrations, my skepticism on whether his phone was operable or not, really was justified. The conversations I'd overheard when I'd passed Bob sitting on his 'Osborn' bench had captivated my imagination and intrigued me. They'd left me asking, although never out loud and always internally, who exactly was Bob? Was Bob an ex-convict, a thought ignited by some words he'd uttered as I'd walked by one morning, "yeah that guy, the guy who was in the next cell', or was Bob ex-military, again, words, just words, "we gave it to them big time when I opened up with my M16 rifle"

I'd decided it was time for me to find out. Figuring out how to approach

Bob was my only concern. Homelessness is an extremely territorial affliction, and infringing on a homeless person's space is sacrosanct to outright intimidation, not that for one moment I believed Bob to be a violent person. I'd spent a week being homeless in San Francisco many years back and I knew full well how to talk to and how to begin the conversation process with most of the people I'd met up there, (read Cardboard City by Alan Zoltie), but Bob would be a different kettle of fish, not only because I wasn't just another homeless person living on his dreary streets, but because I was a 'normal' looking guy out walking and listening to sports programs through the pair of expensive and obtrusive Air Pods dangling from each of my ears. No, this would be a challenge for other reasons. I'd reached the conclusion that Bob had some serious mental issues and was perhaps unstable. I needed to take a tip-toe approach to carve out an opening. I didn't fear him but I was certainly cagey, even though we'd spoken before if only a few words and to carve out the right opportunity to break the ice, took some thought. My mind was in overdrive until I figured out the best way forward, the only way forward. And so, our conversation began, as did our mutual respect for one another and our friendship, and after just a few minutes my admiration for Bob and his amazing story took me into a new world and a new book documenting not only the life and times of my new inspiration Bob, but many others who lived similar lives and who all had stories to tell, stories they were willing to narrate to me, in person and without remorse.

Properly Acquainted

"Bob, how're you doing? I asked, as I crept up on the man's left shoulder, surprising him but not frightening him. Bob's head was turned towards his right shoulder, and without realizing I was there, he quietly swiveled around after hearing my greeting and uttered his surprising calm response,

"Oh well, I'm just enjoying the sun" he muttered, his words spoken in a weird voice, accented against this messy 'hedge' of a beard he shamelessly wore.

"You know who I am, right?" He looked confused, very confused, as if he'd seen me before but couldn't quite remember where? With that in mind, I didn't wait for his reply.

"Bob, would you like me to get you a new pair of shoes?" I said, as I pointed to the old torn up Adidas silver and white sneakers which were clinging precariously to each of his two feet.

"That would be nice" he replied, his demeanor changing instantly and his weird looking round sunglasses sparkling and coming to life, just like his smile, a smile which I'd never witnessed previously.

"My goodness" I said, "it's warm today Bob", I knew his name from other times I'd stopped to give him cash. Each time the amount had varied, from $100 note to just a single dollar bill, but each time he'd graciously thanked me and always followed up with "God bless you, my friend." I continued,

"I saw you sleeping under the tunnel for a few nights last week, you were out of the rain and you looked like you were staying dry."

The previous 3 months had been the wettest in California for about 25 years and each time I'd gone walking at 4 am, something I did every day, I'd seen Bob huddled up underneath his sleeping bag or blankets on the sidewalk inside the tunnel which connected the hill down to the beach from the dog park that bordered condos and the Waldorf Astoria hotel in Dana Point.

His voice cracked into action and this weird accent I'd never heard or detected in any of our previous conversations came barreling out at full volume as he responded. It was kind of New York, Boston, with a childlike drawl. Hard to explain, but very distinctive.

"Well, you know it's been very wet" he said. And then he repeated those same words three times.

"Bob, what shoe size are you?" I asked, as I pointed at the torn-up sneakers on his feet.

In his own inimitable fashion, and drawing out his answer in a manner that suggested he didn't really know, he replied, "Em.. I think 11.5, maybe an 11, but I am a wide, and maybe the widest, but yes, 11 should do it"

"Bob, I need a definitive answer if you can. Are you an 11 or 11.5?" I asked again.

Bob thought long and hard and it became obvious to me the last time Bob was asked this question must have been when he'd been a teenager. It became strikingly clear from the expression on his face that he was slightly confused.

Again, the drawl in his speech and his mild-mannered response took front and center stage,

"Yes, definitely an 11 or 11.5, but very wide" he repeated, leaving me even more confused.

"OK Bob, this is what I am going to do. I will get you an 11 wide and hopefully they will fit. Would you like some new sweaters and a couple of tee shirts too?" I asked.

"Oh no, it should be getting warmer soon, so I don't need them." His answer was concise and to the point this time.

"My worry Bob is that if I bring you new things to wear, someone might just steal them from you. I know what it's like to be homeless and I remember how hard it was to hang on to anything, especially new stuff."

Remembering my own experiences during my week of being homeless in San Francisco, I knew exactly how people behaved when they saw anyone in the same predicament receiving new clothes, new might be the wrong word here because more often than not these clothes were of course used or donated. They would follow the recipients, stalking them closely until they found an opportunity to take what they believed was rightfully theirs. The law of the jungle always ruled.

Bob thought about this and then shook his head, making a negative gesture, suggesting he thought it would be fine.

"I don't want to get you into any trouble Bob, and you know what it's like living rough better than I do, but tell me it's OK and I'll get the shoes."

"It's OK" he said, never smiling and never taking his eyes off his clothes which he'd spread on the grass opposite the Osborn bench.

Changing the subject, I asked, "Bob I detect an accent, where are you from?"

"The Bowery" came his response.

"Manhattan?" I asked, surprised, yet comfortable in the knowledge that I'd kind of guessed he was from someplace around New York. I have a great ear for accents and can guess, 9 times out of 10, where someone originates from. I continued, "That's a very long way from here Bob. How the hell did you end up in California?"

And so, Bob began. The story he was about to tell was not only incredibly sad, but mind-blowingly incredible. A journey of over 50 years, taking him from the East coast of the United States, to the West, all as a homeless person, a vagrant, a bum, as he'd been referred to throughout this journey.

As he was about to begin his tale, a kid on an electric bike zoomed by at 40MPH, just missing me and some of the other people walking on the trail. Shouting at the top of my voice, "SLOW DOWN", Bob said to me, "These kids on those bikes treat me like scum and when I'm sleeping, they come right up to my face spin their wheels very fast and the burning rubber from spinning tires goes right into my nostrils. They hate me. Everyone hates me" He was tearing up.

"I'm nothing but scum to everyone. I'm hated wherever I go and it's been like that since I was a small boy."

"Bob", I asked, "When did you get to California?"

He looked at me and began a completely different conversation.

"Can you do me a favor?" he asked.

"Ask away" I said.

"Can you bring me a steak dinner?"

"A steak dinner?" I replied, "of course I can."

"But I need it cooked a certain way" he continued.

"And what way is that, Bob?"

"Well I am Jewish, and I like it plain with no sauce, no pepper or salt and no spices because I have many allergies. I would love a sweet potato and some corn too."

His mouth was salivating.

"Not a problem Bob, but where would you like this dinner served?" I asked.

"I come here every weekend, to the Osborn bench, and I can be here when you bring the dinner."

Nothing like room service, I thought! But what the heck, I had already offered the shoes, no questions asked, and a steak dinner wouldn't be that difficult to procure for Bob, or would it?

He started to ramble and repeat himself.

"Yes, I was born Jewish, my grandmother looked after me in New York.

I was abandoned at 6 by my parents and have been on the streets or in and out of foster care since then. My grandmother abandoned me too. I don't know who my parents are, I was abandoned" he repeated this several times.

"Didn't your grandmother know who your parents were?" I asked.

"No, she was not my grandmother, but someone I called my grandmother and she couldn't afford to keep me so she eventually abandoned me."

Sometimes when talking with anyone who is homeless, it's hard to differentiate truth from fiction because of the mental illnesses which afflict many of them. With Bob, although I felt some of what he was saying was true, a little voice in the back of my head wasn't so sure. It would be a matter of time before I could trust whether what Bob was telling me, was accurate or pure fiction.

"Yes, abandoned and homeless and I have always been on the streets and I will die on these streets. No one wants me, no one has ever wanted me and there's nothing I have been able to do about that. Always treated like scum, always…" his voice tapered off gently and then, as if nothing had ever been said before, he perked up again, "…could you please make me a steak dinner?"

"Yes Bob, yes I will."

Sometimes Groomed

Dana Point California, is a salubrious and picturesque area. Situated about 3 miles south of the city of Laguna Beach on the Pacific Coast highway, it has become and probably always was, a sought-after city in which to live. Surrounded by a multitude of wealth and opulence which just dazzles, there are homes costing $60 million plus, nestled right on the beach, which, at least to the naked eye, seem to remain empty for 50 weeks in the year and then suddenly occupied when least expected. These homes are large enough to house probably 30 to 40 people, comfortably. Dana Point and its surrounding area also has a very 'surfer' kind of vibe and in complete contrast to these streets of never-ending wealth, there are normal people, or 'surfer dudes and dudettes' who ride around all day and all night on skate boards, or live in old VW vans parked by the side of the road with their surf boards padlocked to the roof of those vans, opposite some of the most expensive real estate on the planet. It's a kind of harmonious bliss, live and let live, and in the 8 years I have lived there I have rarely, if ever, seen any homeless people walking around these majestic streets. If, on occasion a homeless person showed up and camped on the grass or beach, the Dana Point police always seemed to move them along to another, 'less noticeable' area, before anyone fortunate enough to be a resident of Dana Point had a chance to complain about the stench and inconvenience that any homeless encampment might bring. Unlike Santa Monica and Venice Beach, also nice areas, where homelessness is out of control, Dana Point hasn't really seen an influx of these 'unwanted' beings, and for Bob, his territory seemed never-ending, and his audience of prospective donors, untapped. Which was very strange for me. If I was homeless, I would certainly make my way to this city, a city that seemed to be plentiful and safe. There's hardly any crime in Dana Point, and although the cops who work there might disagree with that last statement, from what I've witnessed in other areas of SoCal, the comparison to Dana Point in relation to crime is certainly different. Most of the issues that other cities are experiencing are absent in Dana Point, per say, minor infractions. One might see one or two vagrants walking around now and again, but as I mentioned, they are quickly ushered elsewhere by our noble police force and therefore 'mopped' up before becoming an eyesore. For Bob though, well, he'd been a regular fixture for the past few years, and I was about to find out why and for what reason he picked my neck of the woods to settle down.

You should also be aware that as I have no medical or mental health training, I was and still am, unable to even attempt a guess as to what's wrong with Bob. I have to tell you that when discussing everyday life with him none of what he related to me over the months we spoke seemed in the least bit fictional and I can stand here today, hand on heart, telling you that I believed every single word of his story. Bob is indeed unique and his journey has been incredible, even though it took many months of coaxing it out of him, so I hope it will give you an appreciation on how lucky most of us are to live a normal kind of life in comparison to the angst that this man has had to go through each day while remembering that Bob is only one of 2.5 million Bob's who are homeless in the United States of America so there are many more Bob's out there with stories that I am sure could be more heartbreaking than his.

"BOB?" I would often question whether or not he was listening to me by shouting his name and snapping my fingers or clapping my hands. He would seemingly drift off into never-never land while he spoke, and then quite often repeat his last sentence more than once. Frustrating though it may have been at the time, eventually, and with patience, Bob would end up spitting out all the details, incredible though they seemed, that I needed to piece his story together.

"I've been abused everywhere I've gone" he began, "abused by care homes, by people in the street, by my grandmother, by everyone. I am always being abused." Bob tended to go on and on about any subject I picked, he would be extremely open and serious about his past, but always repetitive, and patience was always going to be my virtue if I wanted to hear his story from beginning to end. Just to describe Bob in a little more detail. He's a portly man, about 5ft 11" and quite often he will arrive at his bench in a presentable manner. By presentable, I mean showered and partially clean. It's impossible for Bob to be 100% clean and manicured or groomed, he's been on the streets too long for that to happen, but sometimes he'll surprise me by wearing a new sweater or have his scraggly matted hair combed, and his 9-inch beard cleaned. I have no idea how or why he does this, but it's become a feature of our meetings, a pleasant interlude from that stale unwashed homeless odor that he carries around his person. Yes, Bob is rather unique in the way he will arrive looking like he's just been given a complete do over, but yet, on close inspection, he still looks the same, bar some minor adjustments.

"Abused, everyone abused me. I am always being abused" he repeated and repeated again.

"Bob" I said, as I stretched out my arm and passed him a crisp new $20 bill, "does anyone else give you money?"

"God bless you; God bless you" he replied, "well I have a pension"

"You do?" I probably looked as surprised as I sounded.

Bob however changed the subject immediately, back to his current plight.

"It's been raining a lot, and I hate the rain" Bob scowled.

"Yes, do you have a shelter to go to? I asked.

"No, I sleep in the tunnel over there" and he pointed to an entrance which was about 50 feet from where we were conversing. "It's my sanctuary, but these bike kids come and abuse me, and so do other people."

"What do you mean by 'abuse me'?" I asked him.

"I've always been abused………"

And off he went again, as I rolled my eyes in disbelief at the thought that his story would be repeated and repeated and repeated until hopefully he would repeat no more and we could finally move on.

Patience, I told myself, patience.

Finally, New Shoes

Bob's shoes arrived at my home, size 11 wide as promised, all wrapped up in their nice beige box and ready to be delivered in person, for a very special fitting. I had arranged with Bob, when we'd last bumped into one another, to meet him back at the Osborn bench on Easter Saturday at 3 pm. Knowing that Bob had a very confused application when it came to counting days and weeks and knowing also from the first time I'd met him on another Saturday afternoon, he'd believed it to be Monday, I wasn't confident that he'd actually show up at all, but armed with hope and Bob's new shoes, I made my way back to the meeting point filled with a sense of foreboding and realizing that if he wasn't there, there would be no way of contacting him to let him know I'd fulfilled my promise and delivered his new shoes as agreed. Parking my car and taking the shoes from its trunk compartment, I walked eagerly towards the Osborn bench situated about 800 yards from where my car was now safely parked. People, the Easter crowd of beach goers, looked on quizzically as I carried Bob's new shoes in a well-branded box, towards their date with destiny. Part of me was excited to assist in Bob's plight, and part of me just thought it was the right thing to do, no questions asked.

I walked through the tunnel which separated the beach from the park, and made a left at the roundabout on the trail, walking speedily up a gentle slope towards the Osborn bench. I could tell within moments that the bench was empty, no sign of Bob or his possessions, and I stopped dead in my tracks to think. "Where could he be?" I wondered.

Some people were walking towards me, and it turned out they were from Israel.

"You see an old homeless guy anywhere around here while you've been walking?" I asked.

They hadn't, but one of the women noticed the new shoes in their new box and politely asked me, "Did you buy him new shoes?"

I nodded in the affirmative and she smiled, saying 'that's so nice, what a blessing."

"So, no sighting of this man at all?" I persisted. And as they shook their heads to let me know they hadn't seen Bob.

I moved up the trail towards the park in the hope that perhaps he'd picked another spot to rest, avoiding the Easter throngs.

No joy. Bob was AWOL.

For 3 weeks I repeated this same task. I would park, get the shoes out the trunk of my car, walk about a quarter mile to the Osborn bench and look to see if Bob had returned, each time convinced he would be there, yet so disappointed to see just an empty bench without Bob or his gear, anywhere in sight. I was beginning to think that the worst had happened and that Bob would not be returning, praying that he hadn't succumbed to his 60 odd years of living rough on our unforgiving streets, when one afternoon, completely unaware of my surroundings while I listened to talkSport on my iPhone App, there he was, right bang in front of me, carrying his one wheelie case and his sleeping bag and walking in my direction, oblivious and of course, chatting wildly to no one in particular.

"BOB!" I shouted at the top of my voice. He was about 20 feet from where I was now walking. "Remember me?"

His reaction was less than convincing, providing me with the slightest doubt that Bob wasn't one to remember anyone.

I continued.

"Bob, I got your shoes, would you like them"
His New York/Boston drawl began spewing out incomprehensible verbiage which suddenly ceased when a light in his brain seemed to turn on, igniting something inside his memory which told him that I was the guy he'd been waiting for all his life, and within seconds, we were best buddies again.

"Oh yes, wide shoes, you have them?" he asked

"Yes, I have them."

"Where are they?" he said, as he looked into my empty hands.

"In my car, just at the bottom of this path" I told him, as I put my hand on his shoulder, spun him around and tried aimlessly to lead him back in the direction he'd just come. Realizing very quickly that my attempt to guide him towards my parked car was going to be an exercise in futility, I stopped.

"Bob, why don't you wait by the 'Osborn' bench and I will go and fetch them for you." It was a statement, not a question.

"Well, how long are you going to be?" he asked, as if he had an appointment which he thought he was going to be late for.

"2 minutes Bob, just sit there and I will be back."

And off I went, hurrying down that path towards my parked car, excited that Bob had returned and hopeful his shoes would fit and I would be able to sit and chat to him for a few minutes, extracting more of his life story and experiences for my pending book, which I had now decided I would call, Bob The Jew.

Bob waited patiently for me, and I was back within minutes, the beige Nike box which contained Bob's new shoes, cradled carefully under my right arm.

"I was abused you know" he shouted, as I turned that last corner and headed back to the bench where Bob was patiently waiting.

"Here you go Bob" I said, ignoring his repetitious desire to keep telling me about his childhood abuse issues. He'd already told me several times, but Bob didn't care, he just wanted to get it out, again and again, telling the whole world that abuse had led him to this time and to this place, where today, Bob would receive new shoes and perhaps begin a new lease on a life which couldn't get much worse.

"What size are they?" he asked, breaking from his repetitious soliloquy.

"You told me to buy an 11 wide, so that's what I did."

"Wide, they have to be wide. I have a very wide foot, wider than most."

"Yes Bob, they are 11 wide, just as you ordered. Why don't you try them on and let's see if they fit. If they don't, I will return them and get you a larger size."

Bob stood up from his bench, removed one of his dirty, filthy, Adidas silver shoes, shoes which had no laces, from his smelly dirty feet, revealing a worn and not so white thick ankle sock, and then proceeded to sit back down ready to remove shoe number two, when I decided one was enough and said to him,

"Bob, just try this one on and let's see how it feels."

And with that command, I removed the right shoe from the box I was holding, placing it carefully in his hand and hoping that I might feel his appreciation by the way he received it.

Not a chance. He procrastinated, telling me quite bluntly, 'podiatry is a very serious thing you know." I did know but at that point in this performance, frankly, I didn't care. "Just get the shoe on the right foot Bob" I told him, while he struggled like crazy to get his heel into the back of the Nike shoe.

"Here, let me release the laces some more. I think they are too tight." Going on the state of his Adidas shoes, Bob was so obviously not used to having laces. Maybe it didn't matter to him or the way he lived and perhaps having no laces led to a quick getaway for him when he was being harassed? No matter what his issue was, I was determined to assist and while I was loosening his new laced up shoes, Bob just went off on a rant.

"Podiatry can determine one's health." He began, "and if the shoe doesn't fit, it can ruin not only a person's feet, it can hurt their back and legs too. I don't really want that to happen to me. I think these are too small, and podiatry is very important to me." he said. All of a sudden, Bob had a procured a degree in podiatry!

Laces loosened, I handed him the shoe and this time he managed to get it on his right foot.

"Looks good to me Bob!" I exclaimed

His New York accent/drawl, became quite loud and unnerving and for a moment, and all the people who were passing us by ogling this scene of a homeless guy trying on a new pair of Nike's given to him by normal looking person, me, stopped in their tracks fearing something untoward was about to happen.

"Podiatry is important" Bob repeated, "these are not the right size. I am an 11 wide. Did you get a wide?"

I was about to speak again, about to inform Bob that yes, these were an 11 wide and about to show him the box, when I decided to take another tact.

I bent down, just as a sales person would do in a shoe shop and I felt where his big toe was situated.

"Bob, these are a good fit. Try the other one on" I suggested. But Bob was having none of it and after sliding the right shoe off his foot and handing it back to me he began to rant, quietly at first, and then, as his supposed knowledge of podiatry increased, his focus on me became more exaggerated, as did his free-flowing diatribe.

"Bob," I said, "let me get you another pair, a lager pair."
"No I don't want them, it's important my feet are kept healthy and I don't want them." He replied.

I took a look at his feet and wondered what was really going on underneath his filthy dirty socks?

"Are you sure?" I said, and then Bob just lost it.

"People should learn to take NO for an answer. I was abused you know, and no one ever took no for an answer. It's not your place to ignore me when I say NO. I don't want your shoes. I don't want anything and I might not be back here again so do not ask me again."

Well, Bob had made himself clear. I took a step back, put the right shoe back into that beige box and didn't offer Bob the option of exchanging them for a larger size again.

By now, Bob was back sitting on his bench and although agitated, a certain calmness seemed to be arriving sooner rather than later inside his confused mind.

"Bob, it was good to see you. Stay safe and stay out of trouble" I said, as I made my way back to my car, shoes in hand, and rather confused, although not surprised, by what had just happened.

"I was abused you know" were the words that I heard as I turned the corner and walked through that tunnel which would take me back to my car in the parking lot. Another day in paradise vying with another human being with a sad case of mental illness. 'Oh, what a world we live in', I pondered, knowing I'd tried to change one man's life, for the better I thought, only to fall short at that last hurdle, but never to give up. Bob was just one of millions who suffered a similar fate, millions who might never recover, but millions who should never have been in this state in the first place.

Madge the Catholic.

She lay there, stone cold, in the heat of the day, well, not the heat, but the middle of the afternoon, because this was a particularly chilly day for southern California, not that the temperature really mattered.

As I walked past her still body which was spread flat on her dirty smelly blanket, right in the middle of the path which wound its way around a public golf course, my instant reaction was 'she's dead, call 911'. She seemed to be just another statistic, another tragedy, another drunken bum, committed to killing herself with excess vodka and little regard for her own existence or soul. The number of empty vodka bottles spread around her lifeless body said it all. Her tipple of choice had become her lethal injection and now, as that warmish sun hovered over both of us and with no other human in sight, my fingers poised over the 911 numbers on my phone, I decided to give her a little kick on her legs, just to be sure that all life had completely drained from this unfortunate woman. It was around 3.30 PM and strangely enough, she wasn't going to be the first person I'd reported dead on this trail. This would be the 3rd, and all in the space of 12 months. I was beginning to feel cursed.

My foot tapped her right leg. Nothing. No reaction. I was reluctant to bend down and grab her wrist to feel for a pulse, don't ask me why, I just wasn't happy about lifting up the arm of a dead woman, especially one I didn't know, and so I tried again, this time a slightly harder kick into her tummy.

Just like the engine on a car or truck which hadn't been started for a very long time, this half-dead person sprung into life again. With a cough and a spurt and a few choice drunken induced swear words, Madge (as I was later to find out her name), sprung to life in the foulest of moods and absolutely clueless to where she was or what she was doing in this quietly serene part of California.

"What the fuck!!!" she growled, "Who the fuck are you? Are you taking my vodka?" "Fuck off and leave me alone, just FUCK OFF!" She was shouting at the top of her voice. Even the crows were making a B-line for another part of the golf course, unwilling to put up with this woman's tirade.

"I thought you were dead!" I told her, as I backed off, ready and willing to exit the scene of a yet unfinished, if self-perpetrated, crime.

Continuing to talk, but knowing anything I was going to say would probably make little if any sense to her, I remarked, "perhaps you should move to another spot where you won't scare off the locals?"

"Just fuck off" then she paused, 'go on, fuck you and fuck off" she insisted.

Standing my ground, I shot back, also in full voice, "NO, YOU FUCK OFF!" at which point she stopped talking, looked at me with what I could only describe as pure amazement, and opened a bottle of her precious vodka, took a quick swig, and laughed, right in my face.

"Who the fuck do you think you are?" she asked me.

"Who would you like me to be?" I replied.

"Can you give me some money?" she said, meekly.

"NO!" and I began to walk away.

"Hey, you!" she screamed, "don't leave me here, I need money"

"Not my problem. I need peace and quiet and you're not helping" I laughed.

"You talk funny" she barked. "What's your name?"

I was the sober one, I thought, and she was the one talking 'funny', in her weird and drunken voice-slurried manner. Our conversation, if you could call it that, continued.

"Alan, what's yours?"

"Madge, and I hate it!" she exclaimed.

"I am here to help you, Madge, and if you decide you want help, then let me know, otherwise I have things to do and places to go, so make a decision and if you're not interested in any help, I will disappear and you'll never see me again!" At least that was my hope. One never knew who was going to show up around these parts. Normally things in Dana Point California were very ordinary and without too much drama. Madge, however, had changed that dynamic in an instant, and here I was, in full conversation, if one could call it that, with a drunk, half dead woman, who was interested in my money, my ability to provide more vodka and my offer of conversation, but certainly not my willingness to assist her in getting off the streets and into a shelter for the night.

It was now 4 pm and I had other things to do.

"Listen" I said, as I pointed a finger at her, from a distance, of course. "I am leaving now, but if you can remember to come back here at this time tomorrow, let's say, 3 pm, (knowing she had no idea what the real time was), I will bring you something to eat, but I will not bring you vodka."

She was silent for a moment and then, without acknowledging my offer, she blurted out, "I like chicken, fried chicken", as she took another swig from her bottle of vodka and lay back down on her blanket, staring drunkenly into the clear blue skies above her, chatting aimlessly to a God who might as well have been an alien from another planet.

Incoherent though it may have been, one or two words drifted in my direction as I retreated up the slope towards my parked car. "Why the fuck do I even matter?" This was the only complete sentence coming from her mouth that I managed to fully comprehend.

Day 2, same time, same place, better weather, no chicken.

As predicted, at least by me, Madge never showed. I presumed she'd be lying drunk someplace else, perhaps the beach or maybe just in another city, but no matter what she'd decided to do, for me, she was a no show, and just like Bob, reliability was a thing in her past, if ever at all.

I walked on up that path towards my car, resigned to the fact that Madge was MIA, when suddenly, out of the corner of one eye, I saw, what looked like Madge, kneeling on the grassy verge just a few hundred feet from where I was headed. It looked like she was praying. She WAS indeed praying, her hands making the sign of the cross against her chest, so obviously a Catholic.

I let her finish, which took more than a few minutes, and as I waited patiently, pondering my next move, some people passed me on the trail, all of them with their eyes transfixed on the scruffy homeless woman kneeling in the grass, hands clasped and praying to Jesus. It was quite a surreal sight and one that would be hard to imagine if not witnessed in person. The Holy Spirit was mentioned out loud more than just a few times and eventually Madge picked herself up from where she knelt, crossing her chest one more time, then standing and tilting her head up towards the sky as if she was asking God personally to do her a favor. God was being treated with kindness and such reverence, and even though Madge now found herself in such dire circumstances, her belief and her trust in the Almighty shone though like a beacon on the darkest of nights, quite the juxtaposition, I thought. To place fate in the hands of the great immortal, to be guided by a light you would have presumed had been extinguished long ago, was the utmost challenge for most who found themselves in a similar position to Madge. For her though, it seemed like salvation, her only chance of redemption and her ultimate sacrifice, to believe in something that had treated her so poorly and brought her to this place on this day with nothing other than her faith.

"Madge!" I shouted, "I've been looking for you."

"The man who talks funny" she replied. "What do you want?"

"I don't want anything, it's you that wanted something."

"You bringing me vodka? You got any money?"

"I already told you Madge; I will bring you something to eat and that's all you're getting. Where do you sleep at night? Why are you in Dana Point?"

"You talk too much" she said.

"Well, I have been told that many times, but not when offering kindness to those in need"

"And what's that's supposed to mean?" she asked.

"It means, what would you like to eat and I will go and get it for you?"

She looked at me, all over, sizing me up and obviously deciding inside her own being whether she could trust me or not. I had seen this move many times when chatting with other homeless people, all of them concerned that I was about to do something to them that would make their dire situation even worse than it already was. Madge was 'casing the joint', and I was that joint.

"KFC" she said abruptly.

"OK I can do that. You stay here and I will be back in 30 minutes, but I am telling you now, if you are not here when I return, this will be the first and only time I bring you food. Understand?"

She nodded.

"Is there anything at KFC you would like that I might not know about?" I asked her.

"No, just anything you can get me would be great." She was beginning to soften. I could tell from her teary eyes that gratitude was definitely there and her only way of depicting that gratitude was to offer some sadness in her reflection that once, just a few minutes ago, had portrayed bravado and a 'couldn't care less, who the fuck are you' attitude.

"Promise me you will be here when I get back and I will leave right now. KFC isn't that far from here so it won't take me long" I told her.

"No vodka?" she smiled.

"Madge, you and I might become friends in the coming days, weeks or months, but rest assured, the only thing I will not buy you, ever, is alcohol and drugs. Do we understand one another?"

She nodded. I continued.

"God would not be happy if you killed yourself with either. Would he?"

She nodded again, this time left to right and not up and down.

I left her on that grassy bank and made my way back to the car and drove as quickly as I could to KFC, a distance of about 3 miles. I hoped, with all my heart, that she would be there when I returned.

Armed with a family meal bucket, I parked again at the beach parking lot, and taking the KFC carrier back filled with piping hot, delicious fried chicken, I marched at double pace towards that grassy bank where I's last seen Madge. To my delight, she was waiting patiently for me, arms and legs relaxed in their squat position.

"Hey, you made it!" she shouted, and I could see from the smile on her face that she was quite excited I'd returned.

"I did indeed, and this is for you" I said, as I put the carrier bag down in front of her.

"Will you share it with me?" she asked.

I didn't know what to say. This was her food, not mine but honestly, I didn't have the heart to say no.

"Sure" I replied and sat down on the grass next to her. I took all the food, napkins and plastic knives and forks from the carrier, spread them all out on the grass and opened up all the food containers. Her face was just a peach and filled with happiness and the aroma of the freshly fried KFC wafted into her nostrils.

"Haven't had this for years" she said, as she picked up a chicken breast, ignoring the utensils, and began swallowing the meat as if she hadn't eaten for months.

"What was the last time you had a meal?" I asked.

'3 weeks ago," she replied.

"How do you survive Madge?"

As she ate, her face was covered in crumbs of batter which had fallen off the chicken and landed unceremoniously on her chin. Crows and other birds, such as seagulls, had gathered about 20 feet from where we sat, all drawn in by the possibility of a random feeding frenzy. It seemed to me at that point in time very poignant that the whole world was starving, and not just Madge.

"I came from San Francisco" she began, "brought here by circumstance, and love. Can you believe that? Love! Ha! What a joke. There's no such thing as love, unless you call loving Jesus and unconditional love, but the love of the great unknown. God's son, sparkling up there in heaven and looking down upon all of us, probably with some disdain."

Madge's vocabulary was certainly above her station, although that thought seemed harsh, categorizing Madge when I didn't even know her. I let her continue.

"Jesus, ah Jesus, my unknown savior. I know one day he will give me a reason for placing me where I now sit, but for now, I certainly don't understand what I did to deserve this." She was now tearing into an ear of corn, with the seagulls getting closer and closer as each nibble produced two stray pieces onto the now, crumb covered grass. Madge was enjoying her feast, savoring every bite and very happy to chat.

"How'd you end up on the streets?" I asked, noticing the many people now walking past us and just staring at this seemingly incomprehensible scene. Me, nicely dressed and sitting watching/talking to Madge, who was dressed in her old torn clothes, a sweater that was ripped, a pair of jeans filled with holes and shoes that I would only place in trash can, and not on a pair of feet, even if those feet were unwashed and dirty.

"What does it matter to you?" she said, angrily.

"I'm curious. I wrote a book about homeless people and I have worked with the homeless for more than 35 years, so every story, no matter how mundane it might seem to you, is interesting to me" I told her.

"You use big words!" she smiled.

"Big words are for small people" I replied, "I speak plainly and truthfully."

She nodded.

Her KFC was hitting the spot and color was now quite evidently returning to her cheeks. Madge seemed to be enjoying this meal and with that contented look, she stared up into the sky again and said,

"In Jesus I trust."

The she looked at me and began to tell her tale, a tale that at first seemed all too common for people like Madge, but a tale nonetheless, filled with heartache, angst and diabolical mistreatment. Just like many others who were homeless, Madge was there by default and of course, not by her own choosing.

"I was once a nun" she began, obviously spurred on by the quizzical, if not, astounded look on my face, "yes, you heard me right, a nun. But that was a long time ago, a time when I never swore, never had sex, and really never talked much, unless I was praying to God and my savior Jesus Christ. Those were the days I would wake up, drink a quick glass of water, say my prayers, eat modestly, pray again and then help those who were less fortunate than me. Days which I recall as being the best days of my life, or so I thought."

"What happened?" I interrupted her as she was biting into another chicken wing.

"Life happened. I was used, abused and then kicked to the curb by the only person I believed I could trust implicitly, and by the time I was 'ejected' from my calling, I had no place to go, nowhere to hide and no chance of surviving any place other than these streets. I grew up in Oregon and moved to California when I was 18. I came here to college but ended up becoming a nun by following my heart when I realized college wasn't for me and that religion was to be my only path. Seems crazy how life treated me back then, but in my heart, I knew that I was here to serve God. I, along with my family, had an incredibly religious and pious upbringing, and it has always been ingrained in my soul that taking the 'God' route was the only path to my salvation. You know how it is though? You get to 15 or 16, start experimenting with drugs, cigarettes, alcohol, and boys and then things change. College then became a priority, and a move to California, where I expected to study at San Diego State and then become a marketing guru. But, shit happens, and on my first day at SD State, I was raped, brutally, and cast aside by the authorities, who didn't for one minute believe me when I was quizzed for hours by the cops and by the school hierarchy. The 'football' player, the culprit, was on a full scholarship and everything I told them was deemed as a lie and everything he told them, the truth, and after hours of interrogation and not one person siding with my side of this horrible experience, I got up the next morning, packed up my things and headed to the Discalced Carmelite monastery, which I knew was only a short ride from campus. And there, welcomed like the holy spirit himself, I stayed for the next 17 years."

"Wow!" I exclaimed, that's quite a story.

"Oh, that's just the beginning. If you want to hear the best part, the next 20 years, you better be prepared to bring me vodka!" she laughed.

"Madge, no vodka, but I am happy to feed you daily, if that's OK?"

"I need vodka, and I also need food. It's your choice. If you don't bring me it, I will just keep stealing it or spending my hard-earned begging money on it. Please help me out" she begged.

"Nope, I won't entertain buying you alcohol or drugs or anything else you don't really need." I said, as I got off the grass and began to walk away.

"Hey, hey you!" she shouted, she still didn't know my name, "Food will do it. You know where I am, come back with food. I eat anything, anything but fish"

"Not even on Fridays?" I shot back, remembering Catholics don't eat meat on Fridays.

Madge laughed and replied, "Fridays I either starve or eat carrots."

I continued to walk to my car, deep in thought and mired in sadness that someone so young and bright and with an incredible future ahead of her, had been reduced to this alcohol infused mess of a woman, left to rot on the side of a grassy bank in the heart of Dana Point California, with no friends or family to save her from the inevitable, a long slow death, where no one knows your name, your age your likes and dislikes and more to the point, really don't care on iota if you live or die.

Two days later, Madge was sitting in the same spot, knees on the grass, head pointed towards the sky, deep in prayer, or at least seeming to pray.

I waited, patiently, until she was finished, knowing all the time she could tell I was watching her. Her eyes kept opening for a quick but subtle look all around her, and I began to believe that all this praying was just a simulation to attract 'givers' and not haters. Homeless people have a tendency to find their place in society and lure in those with cash who are prepared to give. Once that homeless person realizes the best way of attracting a continual cash flow, they stick with their proven method until it runs dry. Madge obviously, well, obviously to me, thought that simulated prayer worked, not that she was faking it all the time, but maybe, just maybe, some of the time, in the hope that people like me would stop by, take pity and donate to her cause, thus relieve, if only for a short while, her angst and destitution. People like to give, and so does their conscience. Giving to a religious person is not always on everyone's list of things to do, but a homeless religious person? Well, that seemed to work for Madge, and going by the pile of cash she had lying next to her, her ploy was working a treat.

She looked up again, this time directly into my eyes.

"You're back" she said.

"Yes, I am, and so are you!" I smiled.

"Bring me KFC?"

"How's that possible Madge, I never know if you'll be here or not."

"Well, I am here, so where's my chicken?"

"Same place as last time." I replied.

"Wanna pray?" she asked.

"Sure" I said, "who are we praying for?"

"The world" she said, and as she uttered those two words I realized, she'd started crying.

"Come on Madge," I told her, "snap out of it, I promise it can only get better" As I said those words, I knew they were meaningless and ridiculous and that I should have just kept my mouth shut.

"When I was in the convent," she began, "I always thought the same thing. Life can only get better, but I was so mistaken, and it only got worse. I gave them nearly 20 years of my life and never asked for anything. When I needed them, the only time I ever needed them, they gave me nothing in return."

"Is that how you ended up on the streets?" I asked.

"I am a good Catholic, at least I was back then, and now, perhaps I am just a little less well behaved, but when the crunch came, I was discarded like a priest who'd been caught with his cock inside a little boy. In fact, that priest was probably treated better than I was. They didn't like my ambition, my ambition to be more progressive and seek connection to the modern world and so, after careful thought and very little discussion, I was told, quite unceremoniously, that my future perhaps lay elsewhere."

"They evicted you?" I asked.

"Yes, and quickly too. Obviously, there was a lot more going on that I've just mentioned, but I had had enough of their hypocrisy, I had enough of the abuse from the male side of the church and I had enough of the way I was being treated. They called me the lepper of San Diego. Not to my face, but behind my back, which hurt even more. If they'd brought their concerns to me directly from day one, things could have worked out a little differently, but they hid their feelings and congregated in private as a daily quorum, just to plot my demise."

"But you still haven't told me what it was you did that was so wrong?" I told her.

And it seemed, by the look on her face at that precise moment, that she never would.

"I need KFC" she said once again, to which I replied, "I needs, get nothing!" And we both laughed.

I could tell, by the look on her face, that my time with Madge was coming to an end and that she was about to retreat back into her insular self. I bid her farewell and hoped that sometime in the next couple of days I would get the chance to interact with her again and find out exactly how she ended up on these streets. Alas, after several attempts at trying to locate her, or her trail of vodka bottles, I never saw Madge again, indeed, it worried me that she just vanished, but hey, that's homelessness for you. One day they are there, the next, gone. There was nothing to keep them in the same spot and most of the homeless people I knew or had met in the past, if not affiliated to a particular shelter, would just roam the streets, finding a place to settle for a few days, and then just move on to wherever took their fancy. It was a vicious cycle and also a game, trying to stay ahead of the inevitable and trying hard to grind out every penny from every local resident in the hope of feeding whatever habit or desire kept them alive or wished them dead. Madge was a number, not a human being. One of millions who had similar issues and found themselves in similar circumstance with little hope of ever retrieving what you and I would call a 'normal' life. I knew in my heart she'd gone, but I never gave up hope of meeting her again. That hope would eventually peter out to just a memory, but hope rarely, if ever dies, and with Madge, hope had hit an internal nerve in my own psyche, a nerve that still lingers to this very day.

Dave the Mormon

It was 2.47 pm on a bright sunny Saturday afternoon, and as kids and adults alike rode their electric bikes up and down the same trail, yes, that very same trail where Madge had appeared from nowhere in particular, and as many weekend warriors trudged towards their favorite beach spot carrying deck chairs and massive cooler boxes filled and brimming with food freshly prepared at home or purchased from one of our many local restaurants, all to be enjoyed as they watched the sun set to the west over the Pacific ocean on another glorious Southern California afternoon, there he lay.

Dave, as I would later find out his name, was not quite on the trail and not quite off it. He was sort of half and half and as he lay. His legs were spread out into the path of all oncoming traffic, bikes and people alike, his head finding a clump of grass to use as a pillow offering him some kind of comfort I suppose, although there seemed to be nothing comfortable that I could see in Dave's sleeping position. Yes, he was fast asleep, and with the whole world passing him by, most of whom didn't give a hoot about who Dave was and why he'd suddenly appeared on what they, as the 'entitled', claimed was their path and no one else's. Again, this was Dana Point, home to the very rich and often famous, and homeless people were seemingly a new phenomenon in this area, a spectacle to be avoided at all costs. Although for years there had been surfer types and beach bums, homeless people just showing up like this had rarely, if ever, happened before. Certainly not quite as often as it was happening now and not in the growing numbers they seemed to be increasing by each and every day. Homelessness in Dana Point was either swept away rapidly by a local police force moving them on to other cities or other parts of Dana Point where no 'normal' person dared frequent, or by boredom and the realization that they were better suited to an area like Newport Beach or San Clemente, where 'acceptance' by the locals was more forthcoming. Don't ask why that was, it just worked out that way. Bob the Jew had once said to me, "don't know where I will be in the coming weeks, but I quite like Laguna Beach and I feel at home in Newport." Maybe he had more 'friends' or opportunities there, but I never found out what drove him to either of these alternative spots. Maybe he just liked being transient? Some homeless people do, some don't. Same situation applies to those of us who are not homeless. Some are transient and some people are just home bodies.

I approached Dave. He was all wrapped up in a red blanket covered with white polka dots and he looked dead, absolutely dead.

People walking past Dave at that moment in time just stared down at this poor desolate soul who was fast asleep and being photographed from all angles, mainly by me. I'd found in the past that if I took pictures before attempting contact of any kind, I could tell from looking at those pictures if the body had life in it or not. I was becoming an unfortunate expert at this, having found several dead bodies on the same trail or close by, in the previous 18 months.

Without hesitation, aftver examining the pictures I'd snapped, I decided to wake Dave from his slumber, believing, although not certain, that he was very much alive.

Why, you might ask, would I wake a sleeping homeless man?

The answer is very simple. Quite often homeless people sleep because they are hungry or thirsty and/or depressed or looking for their next hit. I was always of the opinion, mostly taken from previous experiences, that it's better to feed a hungry person than let them lie there and rot. I had done this many times in the past and remembering that I have worked in some capacity or other with homeless people for over 35 years, I honestly believed that was I was about to do was done with the sole intention of being humane and compassionate.

I gave the 'corpse' a slight kick in his side. Nothing happened, no movement of any kind.

I tried again, and this time his eyes opened. Dave was indeed alive!

"Yo!" I said to this very confused looking man, "you hungry?"

Dave looked up at me from his horizontal position on the grass, very much looking like his last day on earth had just been disturbed by the great unknown.

"Am I in trouble?" he barked.

"Trouble?" I said, "no, I wanted to get you something to eat. When was the last time you had proper food?"

"Yesterday" he said, without any hesitation, "but I can always eat another meal. What are you offering?" He was now sitting upright and removing this red smelly polka dotted blanket from around his body. Dave had taken notice of the word 'food' and without hesitation, responded in the manner I thought he might.

"What would you like?" I asked, "and what's your name?"

"Dave" he replied, "and thank you for asking me if I was hungry. Not many people will talk to me when I am sitting around fully awake, never mind when I am sleeping."

"I work a lot with homeless people Dave, and I often feed those in need. I need to ask you though, and I hope you don't mind? What are you addicted to?" Dave face just dropped and that 'guilty as Hell' look appeared instantly, as his half-smile rescinded into shame.

"Meth" he replied, trying hard to hide his despair.

"Listen, I will not judge you Dave, but you need to be open with me here. I want to know if you have any meth on your person or if you're high from your last hit?"

"Why do you need to know that?" he asked.

"If I am buying you food, which I am happy to do, I need to make sure that it's going to be digested and not vomited straight back out onto the street because of your addiction."

It was common practice for meth addicts to eat and puke up the entire contents of their stomachs within moments of the food entering their gut, making purchase of any kind of sustenance that I'd offered to provide a complete and utter waste of my cash and my time, not that I begrudged either, but it made no sense to provide Dave with food if he was going to expel it immediately just because he was high.

"It's been more than 24 hours since I had a hit" he lied. I could tell he was lying as soon as the words left his mouth.

"Dave, do you believe in a God?" I asked.

"I am Mormon, and I used to believe" he replied.

"Dave, look up to heaven, or down to Hell, and tell me which of the two you would rather end up in?"

He looked at me, then turned away, and as he did so, he muttered under his sad breath, "I took meth about 2 hours ago, I think?" and as he said that, he turned away from me and covered himself with his blanket. Security was so obviously the order of that particular moment for Dave and his embarrassment was there for all to see. By this point in time, other 'beach-goers' were kind of stopping in a funny sort of way, by slowing down as they approached Dave and I and then gathering speed again as they decided they wanted nothing to do with a homeless guy and the man in shorts and a tee shirt who was chatting with him. Personally, I couldn't blame them for running away, something I had become use to over the years, but on this occasion, I saw cause for hope in Dave's face and part of me wished that if only one or two of those who ran could just stop and chat and listen and learn, then perhaps the world might not be so elitist and so uncaring.

"Dave, don't hide from me. I do not judge. I just want to make sure I get you the proper nutrition and that you don't end up puking it all over this beautiful golf course. So, tell me what you really want then I will decide what you really need."

Dave looked lost and obviously didn't care either way whether I got him food or I didn't. I could just tell that he had little ability to comprehend what I was asking. "Sandwich please" he whispered, "cheese and turkey and tomato" he continued, 'on any kind of bread and please no mayo."

Dave immediately covered up his whole being, pulling his blanket well above his head and vanishing into his world of torment and reality. Hidden underneath his pain and suffering was his confusion, depicted by his inability to face anyone who could not understand his need to hide under those infernal polka dots.

I decided to walk around the corner to Gelsons, our local supermarket, where I purchased two sandwiches, fully loaded with meats and veggies. Having bought the sandwiches, I sauntered back at a reasonably swift pace to try and find Dave, hoping he'd not vanished into thin air. As I've mentioned before, homeless people have a habit of being there and then not being there, while all the time being very close to where they'd been before. Make sense? Probably not, but I knew the game and the purpose of their plight and was hopeful that if Dave had gone, I would be able to find him by walking around for a few minutes in that same location. Thankfully when I arrived, he was still under his tree and covered up with his blanket.

I kicked Dave gently on his legs and he spluttered into life.

"Here you go Boss" I said, "2 sandwiches for his Lordship" and I laughed. Dave didn't. He was comatose, and/or just ungrateful.

"Thank you" he said, halfheartedly. "God bless you" he added.

"God doesn't need to bless me Dave, he just needs to get you and all the other people like you off the streets and into housing."

"That's never going to happen, and even if it did, most of the people I know out here like being homeless and off the grid. They like the anonymity of living rough."

"Yes" I said," in my humble opinion, and with my limited experience of dealing with homeless people, I would agree with that. I have met many who enjoy living this way and the government seems to support them, even if it's only minimally."

"We live in a fucked-up world" Dave said.

"And how did you become one of those living this way, Dave?" I asked him.

He took a huge bite from the first sandwich and asked me to sit down next to him by motioning in a downward manner with his arm while he enjoyed his mouthful. He had a canister filled with water, which at first, I thought was booze, but after double checking by smelling it, realized indeed, it was plain water and nothing stronger. Washing down each bite with gulps from his canister, Dave began to talk, and talk and talk.

Salt Lake city was his place of birth, born into an average family, living in an average street and attending all the things average people seem to attend. School, without issues, church, obviously the Latter-Day Saints variety, social events and sports, and, this was the kicker, Dave got a job in a hardware store, owned by a church member, when he was 14 years old. The store owner, a very pious and religious man called Steven, treated Dave like the son he never had but always wanted. With 4 daughters, 2 younger and two older than Dave, Steven had begged his wife to allow his daughters to enter the business and to learn his trade, just in case, heaven forbid, something happened to him and the family needed the income when Steven was dead. His wife refused, Dave told me, purely on religious grounds, insisting HER daughters, not THEIR daughters, were too good for his type of work and sighting the Mormon church's point of view that women should be married off to bare children as early and as young as was possible, Steven's wife was determined to offer all of her daughters to the elders, feeling that as 'storekeepers', they would be frowned upon and discarded by those who really counted in that particular community process, leaving Steven with little option but to find someone, preferably a boy/man, to assist him with his daily routine at the store. Dave, as luck turned out, needed to help his own family, and he also had ambitions to one day attend college. He was outside the store, on his way in to purchase some items for his mother when he noticed the ad for a job posted on a sign, stuck 'half-heartedly' and 'crookedly squint' on Steven's shop window. Dave, saw the sign, applied and Steven offered Dave the position on the spot. That day turned out to be the beginning of the end for Dave and all his ambitions, a day that certainly left an indelible scar on the man who, by now, was almost at the end of his first sandwich, and a day that Dave, told me, "Killed my soul and my belief in all that was supposed to be good about life."

My curiosity had peaked as Dave told his story and knowing that in general homeless people don't like to chat for more than a few moments to strangers I decided to take a chance and tell Dave I would be back at the same time the following day to bring him more food and continue our conversation.

"I'm not going anywhere" Dave said, "but can you please do me a favor and bring me some bottles of water when you come tomorrow? The water I use to refill my canister comes from a fountain tap on the beach, and honestly, it's awful."

"Dave" I said, "it would be my pleasure to do that. Anything else, or will you eat whatever I decide to bring you?"

Dave smiled, and didn't say anything. He didn't need to. I could tell from his face that it would never matter what I brought him, as long as I brought him something. I stood up from the grassy verge, wiping off residue dirt and grass from my jeans, and began to walk away.

"Hey!" Dave shouted, "any chance you can get me a bible?"

I shrugged my shoulders and shouted back, "I will try!"

Unfortunately, due to work commitments, I could not return the following day, and fearing I may have lost the opportunity to meet Dave one more time, knowing how transient homeless people can be, I'd never made any effort to grab him a bible from our local book store when I returned two days later. I also arrived, at that same time as previous, without too much in the way of food. I had managed to secure some chocolate and some protein bars, just in case Dave was still around, but as I mentioned, one just never knew what to expect, so I wasn't hopeful that Dave and I would ever meet up again.

As feared, Dave had vanished and my attempt to provide him with some more food, albeit protein bars, failed at its first endeavor. My thoughts turned immediately to where he could possibly be or to a more certain possibility that Dave had now located his being to another part of town. When these situations occur, there's not too much that you can do to find the missing person, even though they are not exactly missing per say. Homeless people have an ability to vanish for months on end only to show up again, and always without warning. Of course, it's always without warning, because no one in their right mind knows where a homeless person, known or unknown to them as a 'local fixture' can end up or disappear to and, let's face it, no one really cares. Putting the protein bars back into my pocket, I started to walk back to my car, all the time looking left and right in the hope that Dave might materialize.

He didn't. I left the parking lot and hoped that Dave might be back in his usual spot on the following day. He wasn't, and in fact it would be a very long time indeed before Dave and I would see one another again. Part of me decided that because I'd never made an effort to get that bible for Dave, God was punishing me by not allowing Dave to finish his story. The other part of me said, 'don't be so stupid Alan, and move on."

I moved on.

Hare Krishna, Hare, Hare!

They came out of nowhere in particular, about 6 of them, dressed in burnt orange-colored robes and with shaved heads, making their way slowly though the center of a town called of San Juan Capistrano, singing loudly.

"Hare Hare, Hare Hare, Mr Krishna Hare Krishna"

If you've never seen these devoted 'bhaktas', found in many cities all around the globe, they always, to me anyway, looked so happy as they sang danced and plodded their way down high streets and leafy lanes with not a care in the world other than complete devotion to their supreme prophet. Each and every one of them certain in their own minds that they would one day be reincarnated and returned to this earth to save another soul, preach to another convert or just simply be allowed to follow the path that their leader had prophesized. When I was a young man in my late teens and I followed the Hare Krishna's around London, I used to mock them, inwardly of course, and really could not understand their complete and utter happiness. They really amused me, in a kind of quizzical way. They never asked, or so it seemed, wanted for anything and as they trod, often bare footed, around London's dirty filthy streets, they seemed to ignore the real world that continued to revolve around them and cared only for their insular beliefs and existence that they so craved. Hare Krishnas, after years of watching them, debating with them at Speakers Corner in Hyde Park London, eventually earned my respect on many levels and their inability to be consumed by materialism of any kind, seem to push them even harder into deeper prayer and contentment. On this particular day in San Juan Capistrano however, while watching the 6 of them chant and sing and dance down Main St, my head was turned by this man walking about 20 feet behind the main group who was also dressed like the Hare's but not participating in either their singing or dancing. It was odd, and something I had never witnessed before, certainly not with any Krishna gathering I had seen in my past. All the Krishna parades I had witnessed consisted of a group who stuck together religiously, danced and sung and handed out Hare Krishna pamphlets always together. This was indeed odd. I hung around and then followed the guys, not knowing where exactly they would end up, but curious enough to see what this particular team was about to do. I didn't have much else to do on this incredibly hot and steamy Saturday lunchtime, and one never knew what patience could bring in the way of entertainment or indeed a learning experience.

Of the 6, really 7 if you counted that one straggler, the only one carrying anything was the guy at the back, the guy 20 feet from the main event. He had, what looked like a bag full of food and clothes and a folded-up tent, all packed neatly and stowed perfectly in balance on a trolly with 4 wheels. He was pulling this trolly very slowly behind him and looking around constantly to check if anyone was going to steal from his packed up 'stash'. Well, that's what it looked like to me, but in all honesty, he might have just as easily been looking all around for people to convert! The other 6 guys, all Indian, were consumed in their own festivities, a party of sorts that they seemed to be enjoying tremendously, even though the song, "Hare Hare, Hare Hare, Mr Krishna, Hare Krishna" was becoming very repetitive and perhaps even a little annoying. Kids and adults alike had stopped doing what they were doing and were watching each and every step these Krishnas were taking and watching with more than just a little curiosity. As they group progressed on their journey to wherever it was they were intending to stop, the crowd grew larger and larger until eventually, out of the blue, a cop car arrived, pulling into the Shell gas station on the corner of the main crosswalk in town. Two cops exited the vehicle, ready and willing to intervene by breaking up the crowd and dispersing the Hares. This was, after all, San Juan Capistrano, home of the famous mission of San Juan and host city of the annual swallow festival held each February, so what were a bunch of unwanted Hare Krishnas doing in a town where nothing perhaps other than the normal, ever took place? The answer was about to be revealed and revealed by a couple of cops who hadn't bargained for what was about to happen.

The Hare Krishna 'squad' weren't causing any trouble, in fact, all that they were guilty of was creating an overflowing interest from bystanders who hadn't seen their likes before, and probably wouldn't ever see again. Obviously, they were looking for handouts from their audience, but unlike most who panhandled for a living their calm and collect mood and ability to be pleasant and unforceful when asking or suggesting that donations were always welcome, stood them in good stead as religiously pious and certainly not aggressive or bothersome. The 'boys in blue', our local police force, decided that 2 of them would not be enough to control the crowd, even though it was peaceful and looked to me like everyone involved was placidly calm and certain this march was only going to last a few more minutes.

Two more Ford Explorer police cars arrived and 4 more cops joined the party. I had this horrible thought that the Krishnas were about to be picked up and booked for disturbing the peace. One of the Hares looked across from the other side of the road where he was dancing and, by the look on his face, realized the police were about to get involved. I knew the police would not stand for any backchat or the slightest suggestion of intolerant behavior, but the Hares suddenly changed tact and began making their way across this busy road, still dancing and singing, and definitely heading directly towards the cops. "What on earth are they doing?" I thought, as I too moved on in tandem with the crowd, who by now were absolutely intrigued and invested in a scene which was about to become rather comical.

Seeing that all traffic around this main crossroads had halted and that gridlock was about to become the order of the day, 2 cops were sent to control the situation and get things moving along while the other 4, (2 of which were female), stood on opposite corners waiting for the party to move on. The Hares, sensing their odds had improved from 6 to 4 cops, danced right across the main road, singing and partying in their own inevitable manner towards the remaining 4 cops and finally reaching the other side of the road and then surrounding the cops, corralling them into a corner while their song played on. "Hare Hare, Hare Hare, Mr Krishna, Hare Krishna." Although they were doing this in a very peacefully and in a non-threatening manner, the 4 cops had their right hands on the top of their holstered guns, ready and waiting, just in case the unthinkable occurred. The cops also looked like they were about to get very pissed off with the Hare's and that at any moment, with the Hare's becoming more and more vocal, this standoff could come to an end in a manner unbefitting to Hare beliefs. Handcuffs and then jail!

The audience laughed, the police didn't, and the Hares just sang. It was a scene from a comic book, an unbelievable intrusion from the mundane to the surreal, but it was happening in real time as I, and many others, watched and it was to say the least, quite amusing.

The cops decided, after the Hares had danced around them for a few minutes, that enough was enough and without too much warning suggested to the onlooking crowd that the party was over and they should disperse immediately. To a chorus of boos, most of the crowd took heed and left the area, but the Krishna boys stayed and ignored all warnings from an increasingly frustrated police presence. And at that moment I saw my opportunity to find out exactly who these Krishna boys were. I had a suspicion they might have been homeless panhandlers, and I had no idea why I thought that, but the 7th Krishna, the one with the 4 wheel trolly, well, he was the giveaway. It didn't take too much to deduce these guys were camping rough and making what they could from begging, to buy food and water and trying to stick to their Krishna beliefs as they traveled to wherever it was, they were going.

The cops had rounded them all up, all but number 7, who was still on the other side of the road. They placed them next to one of their cop cars and as the Hare's singing went up a notch, their rigid police work, finding out exactly who these guys were, began in earnest.

I crossed the road and approached number 7, who, after we got to know one another over the next half hour, would introduce himself to me as, Arkush.

"What's going on Boss?" I asked Arkush, as I approached him head on. At first, I could tell he was rather skeptical and perhaps a little frightened that someone from nowhere just walked up to him and began speaking with him, especially with all the police activity going on across the street with his mates, but after giving him a huge smile and taking out a $5 bill from my pocket, his persona mellowed immediately by the prospect of a pending 'pay-day', as he stared at the money and not at my face.

In his broad and very pronounced Indian/American-English accent, and with his head moving from side to side as he spoke, a movement so typical from most Indian people while they speak and express their feelings, Arkush said to me, "not too much my friend, ve are just making noise, lovely noise and ve are vanting to get some cash to live on for another day."

When he was done speaking he placed both hands together in a 'praying' motion, Just like the emoji on my phone, and brought them up towards his chest as a sign of respect and peace.

I shook his hand and we introduced ourselves. I told Arkush about my time in London and specifically 'speakers' corner' on Sunday mornings where I'd stand listening to the teachings of the Krishna, amused and enlightened at the same time by how peaceful this religion sounded. Arkush agreed and asked me if I would like to join them?
I told him I had more to do with my life than sing the same song all day every day, and then asking him the $64,000 question, "Are you guys all homeless or do you live somewhere."

"No Sir, ve are all very homeless" Arkush said, while his head vibrated from side to side with every syllable uttered.

"Is that your gear for night time?" I asked, while pointing to the 4-wheeler he was dragging behind him.

"Yes Sir, ve alvays have our tent, just in case" he replied.

"In case of what?" I asked him.

"In case ve cannot find a shelter."

"There are very few shelters here Arkush" I told him with some authority.

"I know Sir, ve are sleeping rough right now" he said.

"Well how and why did you come to San Juan if you knew there was no place to shelter indoors?" I asked.

"Ve follow the Hare, and ve go where he tell us to go."

"And he told you to come to San Juan Capistrano?" I asked.

"Yes Sir" was all he said in return.

By now the cops had cleared the crossing and Arkush was about to walk over the road to join his fellow Krishnas.

"Arkush, may I offer you some advice?" I asked.

He nodded in expectation.

"May I suggest you walk down that road over there, Del Obispo, in that direction" I said, while pointing with my right hand, "and in about 2 miles, you will come to the harbor of Dana Point where there is grass, lots of people and plenty opportunity to gain good fortune for you and your team here"

He smiled and nodded and walked away, looking back after each stride to see if I was following him. I was. I was still curious as to why this lot were actually down in this part of the world, and where exactly they'd come from.

Arkush gestured with one finger for me to keep coming and to join him and the rest of the Krishnas, so I did. We were all now gathered on the west side of the street and the signing had ceased. The police had said their piece, calmed the situation down and were about to drive off to solve whatever crimes they had to resolve that day. No one was going to jail and the crowd had dispersed.

Arkush introduced me to his merry bank of worshippers. I was honored that they just accepted me without knowing anything about me, but again, that was the Krishna way. Make friends and influence people, plain and simple. To them, everyone was a possible member, and in reality, I suppose that was true of all religions around the world.

"Guys" I said, addressing all of them at one time, "are you hungry?"

Boy, were they hungry. We hit a local vegan restaurant and while they all waited outside, I walked in and purchased 7 meals for for 7 kings. They devoured their food, not uttering a single word while they ate, and between them, they drank over 5 gallons of water, all in the space of 25 minutes.

"Thirsty then?" I asked.

They all nodded.

"OK listen up, I need to know how you all got here and where you came from?"

"Why?" Arkush asked.

"Good question Arkush, and one I really need to answer, but before I do that, I need you to know that I work a lot with homeless people and I am very interested in helping rid the world of homelessness, no matter how long it takes. Religion to me is secondary, but the stories you guys have might be important in making the homeless crises a thing of the past" I told them.

"In what way" Arkush asked.

"In any way possible. The more people know and respect how hard it is to live on the street, the more chance there might be of an understanding and common goal to stop this madness."

Arkush piped up again and he seemed to be their spokesperson, "He has been brought to us by the Krishna!!"

Arkush was not only addressing his fellow Krishnas, but seemed to be proclaiming this thought to anyone close by who might want to listen. And after this loud proclamation, the signing began again, 'Hare Hare, Hare Hare, Mr Krishna, Hare Krishna!"

It looked to all and sundry that my time with these guys was up and with their bellies full to bursting, they stood up in together as a team, which was how they did most things, all in unison, and taking my advice, headed west on Del Obispo towards the marina, without one iota of a goodbye or thank you.

Joan The Baptist

Each day I saw her, she would just be sitting there smoking her cigarettes, seemingly without a care in the world other than her smokes. She would inhale one after another, probably all day and certainly every day. She had dirty blonde hair which looked like it was washed daily, although I could never figure out exactly where she would come from or go to. Definitely homeless, I presumed, but always carrying a small red wheely suitcase behind her as she trudged up and down Pacific Coast Highway, coffee in her left hand and the telescopic handle which was pulling her case, in her right. She would sit, not uncomfortably, on a stone wall that protruded from the east side of the men's and lady's restrooms in the parking lot at Salt Creek beach. One leg crossed on top of the other, looking aimlessly into nowhere in particular and avoiding it seemed, at all costs, conversation with anyone. She had no phone, no books, no interest in conversation, she just sat. My curiosity had peaked weeks before I'd made my initial approach, but after being told by several of my 'morning walk friends' that the lady was completely unapproachable, with many of them offering to buy her food which she'd politely declined, I was reluctant to make any attempt at conversation just in case I pissed her off and upset the equilibrium of her routine. She looked miserable, but then again, who wouldn't be? Sitting on a wall, walking up and down the same stretch of road each day, no home, no family, no way out? I'd thought to myself several times, 'this lady must be very sad', and perhaps I should make some attempt at conversation, which really never happened until that one fateful morning when face to face contact became unavoidable. Homeless people have always intrigued me. Again, my book Carboard City explains in part why, but their plight and the sadness that accompanies each and every one of them, leaves indelible scars on my fascination and failure to comprehend what it must be like to spend an entire lifetime just walking and living on dirty, empty, crime-infested streets. I did it for a week, but to do it for months, years, decades? What an impossible thought, what a nightmare and what a way to spend time in the short period we all inhabit this planet.

The kids, the ones on the electric bikes, the ones she hadn't noticed, who were approaching her as she walked across the parking lot, didn't give a hoot that she was right in their sights as they sped at 35 MPH while balancing only on their rear wheel, their front wheel in the air and facing the heavens. These particular kids and so many others just like them are the bane of all who walk each day on trails that used to be so quiet and safe until the invention of E-bikes. The bikes, self-powered by an electric motor and so much heavier than a normal pedal bicycle, are ridden by inconsiderate, daredevil teens who don't give a damn about anyone or anything in their path. They terrorize the beach, the trails and even the grassy park that is situated behind that very same parking lot, performing Evil Knievel tricks that often go wrong, but more seriously upset and frighten those who just want to relax and enjoy the solitude of the parks and trails that Orange County has to offer. The sad thing is, no matter how many times they are scolded by adults and other teens to slow down, these 'cyclists' ignored warnings and tellings-off, by returning the criticism with vile language and even more ridiculous stunts and hair-raising acts of speed. Having spoken to the mayor of Dana Point on several occasions, insisting that something needed to be done to remove this nuisance from the trails and parks, to date, when writing this book, the issue has only become worse and there seems no end in sight to this problem being halted by the passing of laws or the implementation and enforcement of speed controls on our trails.

Anyway, these cyclists were barreling towards this homeless lady, knowing full well that if they happened to hit her, her life would probably never be the same again. The weight of these bikes and the speed they were traveling at could more or less strike dead any human being in an instant, but they didn't care. They thought they owned the place, believing no one could or would ever put an end to their irresponsible antics.

"Hey Fuckers!!!" I shouted at the top of my voice, "slow the fuck down!!!"

The homeless lady with the suitcase looked around, moving her head to her left, where I was standing, now aware that three kids were about 12 feet away from her and closing at the speed of light.

Awkwardly, she spun around and fell on her left side just as one of the bikes hopped over her body, the kid riding that bike, managing to 'air' his bike as he catapulted like a trampolinist over her horizontal body while she covered her face and hoped while she prayed that he'd managed to clear her without injuring any part of her being. His athletic or irresponsible ability to make himself 'jump' her body, saved not only the life of the lady on the floor, but also the embarrassment of the kid riding the bike, who, after seeing what had happened, and obviously knowing that he'd done wrong, vanished out of sight in seconds followed by the other two bikes who were have nothing to do with this unfortunate incident and probably realized that the shit was about to hit the fan. The homeless lady, still lying flat on the tarmac, was crying and her case was freewheeling down a slope towards the other side of the parking lot.

I ran towards her, and another passerby, ran towards her freewheeling suitcase.

"Are you OK?" I asked, as I offered my hand to assist her back on her feet.

Tears were running down each cheek and she was obviously in a state of delayed shock.

"Here, grab my hand" and as I held out my right hand, her dirty tobacco stained palm grabbed mine and I helped her to her feet.

"These kids should be banned from riding anywhere other than the streets" I told her.

"Yes", she said, "they are always tormenting me, even when I am sitting just minding my own business."

"Are you OK?" I asked.

"I'll be fine" she replied and as she was patting herself down, just to confirm there were no broken bones or cuts, another lady sauntered towards us pulling the rogue suitcase which had decided to make haste while the whole episode had unfolded.

The lady with the suitcase dropped it and ran. She obviously didn't want a thank you or any kind of conversation, deciding that homeless people were to be avoided at all costs.

"What's your name?" I asked.

"Joan."

"None of my business Joan, but are you homeless?" I said, sheepishly.

"Yes, and I have been this way for many years" she replied.

"How many?"

I received her evil eye and a look that said, "fuck you, it's none of your business", followed by, "too many to count and no end in sight" Joan said, as she took hold of her case and began the short walk back to her seat at the edge of the restroom building.

"Joan I am Alan and I work a lot with homeless people. I also wrote a short book about going homeless in San Francisco."

"You're homeless too?" she asked.

"No, but I was, but only for a week. Worst week I ever had." I told her.

"It's no fun and I hate it but I have no place to go"

"I see you every day. I see you walking up and down PCH."

"Oh, yes, I make sure I get something to eat each day and I find shelter at night."

"Where's the shelter?" I asked her.

"Now, that's another story, and one that will take me a while to explain."

"Would you like me to get you some food?" I offered.

"Yes please" she said, "I love Micky D's, is there any possibility we could go there?"

Well, there was, but there was also no way in Hell I would put this lady in my car. First of all, I didn't know her, and secondly, she stunk to high heaven from all those years on the streets. My car was newish and I didn't need to take the chance that her presence would make it smelly and dirty.

"Let me shoot down the road and get you what you want and I'll bring it back. Would that work?"

"Marvelous" was all she could say, and as her tears dried up, the anticipation of a meal, more of a feast, changed the color of her face and brought a smile back to where the tears had just dried. Joan was excited, and I could tell she was keen for me to get going.

"Bless you sir" she said, 'and may God have mercy on your soul."

"Joan I am not dying here; I am just going to get you a burger!" I laughed.

"McNuggets too please!!!" she shouted.

"Deal" I said, 'I will return in ten minutes so don't leave"

"Emmmm, where would I go?" She looked around and laughed and as she did so, I walked up to my car, got in and drove off to McDonalds.

Returning some 25 minutes later, armed with three bags filled with food, I sat down next to Joan, tempted by the fresh smelling food that aromatically punctured the air between Joan's disgusting homeless scent and my very uncomfortable sitting position. I had no idea how she managed to sit in this same spot all day, every day. If it were me, I would have ventured 35 yards further down the hill towards the bank of grass that bordered the sand and trails. Any thoughts I had of offering Joan that same moving advice vanished with her next sentence.

"I like it here, here in this spot" she said.

"Why's that Joan?" I asked.

"What's your name?"

"Alan."

"My pastor was Alan."

"Where was your church?"

"Yes, Alan, he was a nice man, and his sermons were fabulously interesting." As she said this, she seemed to be drifting off into deep thought, her past so obviously taking over her semi-conscious state. "I recall so many of his words of wisdom, one in particular, when he mentioned that our trial is life itself, and judgement will be honored in heaven by God the judge, who will in turn, judge no one other than the guilty"

"Very nice" I told her, "But where was your church?" I asked again.

"So, what did you get me to eat Pastor?"

Ignoring her wish to associate my name with her former pastor's name, I pulled the bags from the ground and opened all 3. There were at this point in time, perhaps 5 or 6 other people milling around the restroom building, some waiting to relieve themselves and standing in a short line to enter the lady's room, and some waiting for friends who were either in that room or driving their cars around looking for a parking space. All however were oblivious to Joan and I and the conversation we were having, but some were obviously jealous that I had three bags filled with delicious fast food, and although their gaze was centered on the bags of food, you could tell that their minds were focused on the wonderful smell the food had created on the sea breeze.

"I will have that one!" Joan declared, as she picked out a small box which contained a double cheeseburger, "oh, and I LOVE their fries. I have always loved their fries. They're the best."

Joan had a broad smile on her face and was so obviously enjoying her new found bounty.

The burger came out of its box and Joan began to devour it, but not in the way one might expect, she devoured it by nibbling around the edges and leaving the center as the main event. She was wrapped up in her glory, burger in one hand, fries in the other and a smile that read, contentment.

"Good?" I asked her.

"Delicious!" she replied, as she licked her lips and smiled as if she'd just won the Lotto.

And as Joan drifted off into her past, a sign so evident, just by the look on her face, I decided it was time for me to exit left and leave her with her feast, in the hope that on another day, Joan would remember this moment and our conversation, and allow me to learn more about her plight than I had on this particular day.

I rose very quickly, quietly and without too much fuss and walked back to my car. Joan was consumed by her food and hardly noticed I'd left. At least that's what I thought as I started my car and drove off to spend another night in my luxurious home.

Two days passed, and as I came back from my 10 mile walk towards my car, I heard a voice coming from behind me and shouting, "where did you go?"

"Joan!" I exclaimed, "how are you?"

"You left me" she said, in a very serious tone.

"Joan, I would never leave you. You were enjoying your food and I thought it best to let you savor it without my incessantly questioning your past" I told her.

"My past doesn't exist, it's only my present and future that's certain" Well, I thought, that's a rather philosophical way to look at things.

"Joan, the future is always uncertain, so why do you think your future is already carved in stone?" I asked.

"God has his plan, and his plan for me is set in stone, as you say, and that plan was to abandon me into this life of desperation and despair, with no family, no friends and certainly no prospect of ever leaving this horrible existence I live."
"Well I hope that's not the case Joan, and I hope we can try to propel you in the right direction."

She continued,

"Do you think I enjoy eating fast food, leftovers, trash can remnants, and all the other cast offs that people discard, rich people, not poor people, and do you think I honestly believe there's an end in sight to my misery? Ha! You have to be joking. I have been abandoned. I have been left to rot, not only by society, but by my religion and by God himself, providing of course God is a he!"

"How'd you end up on the streets?" I asked once again, hoping that this time I would receive and answer.

"You really want to know?" she said.

"Well, I've asked you several times now, so hopefully, when you're comfortable, you'll tell me. I am interested to learn more about you."

"Why? What am I to you? Why would you care?" she asked, again, in a perfunctory dislikable tone.

"Joan", I tried to remain calm and not to talk down to her, "I am just as human as you, I may be more fortunate, but I am a human being, and every human deserves respect. If you don't want to tell me it's fine, and I promise I won't ask again, but know this, sometimes when the truth comes out the healing process can begin and you just never know what another human being can do for you when they know who you are where you've been and what you need."

My speech over, Joan began to think. I could see the cog wheels churning inside her head, deciding if she should shut the conversation down or just spill the beans. I waited, and she waited.

"Well, if I begin to tell you, it will take some time. How much time do you have?"

"Honestly, not long, but I am here every day and I'm happy to speak with you and learn about you piece by piece, let's just say instalments are fine, and I will trade you stories for the foods of your choice."

Joan took out a pack of Marlboro cigarettes, lit one, looked at me and said, 'Would you please get me some breakfast?"

I smiled and made my way across the parking lot to a French café called Moulin, where I ordered a croissant and coffee for Joan, and a bottle of Orangina for me.

I sat down next to her, gave her the food and waited. This time she seemed more open to chatting and as she took her first bite of the croissant, her story began.

"1972 I moved with my family from Detroit to Los Angeles, I was 15. My parents were devout Christians and my dad was a preacher. They opened a new church in Simi Valley and he was given the job of being it's first minister. Baptists through and through, religion ran my life for the next ten years, making me the most miserable young lady in town. I hated it, hated the rigmarole, the rigidity and my inability to mix and socialize with people my own age. I was 17 when a member of the 'congregation' raped me and 18 when I had my first abortion."

She puffed on her cigarette and took small bites from her croissant as she spoke and the words became clearer and more horrifying the more she ate and the more she smoked.

"At 19 my parents threw me out because they found marijuana in my bedroom and at 20, they took me back because my dad got sick and being their only child, my mother needed the help. At 21 I was raped again, and at 22 I tried to kill myself." Tears were rolling down her cheeks as she related these events 'machine-gun style', one after another, like a shopping list.

"When I was 23, my parents died in a car crash, leaving nothing other than the clothes they wore and the bible they prayed from. I ran from Simi Valley, moved in to an apartment in LA and got a job working as an assistant to one of the senior VPs at a well-known record company. I had no degree, but I was good with numbers and with organizing his schedule, and we got on great. He was a true gentleman, and he loved the fact I was a Baptist, as was he. Over the next two years I was as happy as I'd ever been, so happy in fact that I decided to find religion again, having vowed never to re-enter any church after my parents died. I even went back to the Baptist way of life, just for a short while, hoping in my heart that by doing so I was honoring my parents and all they'd believed in." Joan looked at me, just to make sure I was listening, and then continued. "That's when everything changed, everything, my whole life. But that's all I am saying today, so if you bring me breakfast or lunch or dinner tomorrow, I will tell you more. Deal?" she said.

Well, going on my past performance record, the chances of her being there again were slim to zero, but hey, you just never knew when and where homeless people, the most transient people I have ever met, would end up. One day they were there, the next, gone.

Joan seemed genuine in her promise to hang around and with that in mind, 24 hours later, there I was, croissant in hand and coffee at the ready. Perched in her usual spot, was Joan.

"OK, you persuaded me to bring you more, and here it is" I said, as I handed over her breakfast.

"Thank you, young sir" she said, as she tipped her head formally in my direction. She was acknowledging me as if I was her superior, and I didn't like that one little bit. We are all human and all equals and while I admire respect, I dislike people with a superiority complex and also an inferiority complex. Joan, I decided, was just being respectful, and I made no comment on her requirement to bow in reverence, giving her plenty time to unwrap her goodies while I took my place next to her, ready and willing to listen again.

I began by reminding Joan of where she'd left off the last time we'd spoken. "You were about to tell me how your life changed forever after you went back to being religious"

"Ah!" Joan said, "you have a keen memory!"

"Yep, always did have and hopefully always will" I said, trying to humor her as she sipped on her coffee.

"The job at the record company in LA gave me an insight to the good and the bad of the record industry, and I had the chance to meet many famous rock stars in the flesh and up close and personal. Often, they would ask me out and at that time in my life, I was 24 years of age and I was also very attractive and really interested in meeting new people, especially those famous ones who frequented our offices all the time. I was captivated by their ability to create music and commercialize it so everyone loved it. I'd become a music junkie of sorts. I loved everything, from country to rock to classical and my boss, the other staunch Baptist in my life, encouraged me to progress through the ranks at that company, in the hope that one day I would achieve a more senior position doing something more than just being someone else's skivvy. One thing led to another and my boss, the Baptist, began taking more than just a liking to me as his work colleague and although I knew he was married, I began this magical affair with him that led me to believe for the first time in my life, I was in love!"

Joan had finished her food by now and her coffee cup was about to be discarded as the dregs of that beverage entered her mouth, clearing out the contents of the cup and finally she discarded it in favor of yet another cigarette.

"Joan where do you get the money to buy cigarettes?" I asked her.

She ignored me, preferring to blow smoke in my face and resume that pensive look I had grown to know and hate.

"What an affair we had," Joan continued, "he took me all over the planet, in first class I might add, and we used to have late dinners together, great sex and the promise of more to come when he left his wife, which of course never happened."

"Did he have kids?" I was prying now.

"I believed everything that man told me, trusted him, implicitly, but deep down, well…." She paused. "Come back tomorrow," Joan blurted, "I'll tell you more." She winked at me, as if to say, 'I am not telling you anything until you ply me with more food'. Joan was no fool and it seemed by this very direct statement that I was no longer welcome. Joan took another draw from her, almost finished, cigarette, looked the other way, as if to say, FUCK OFF, and then blew her smoke towards the beach, which was then immediately blown back into my face by the sea breeze. 'I guess my questions would have to wait?', I thought, as I took out my key and walked once again back to my car.

Eat, sleep and repeat. That's the feeling I was beginning to have with Joan, and as I pulled up to the café to buy her breakfast once again, it felt weird to think

I was becoming her bitch. Bags in hand, I parked up and went to look for Joan. She was nowhere to be found. Vanished, gone and just like everyone else who is homeless, there was no way to track her, call her of even go to an address where she might be. Perhaps, I thought, she'd be back tomorrow?

My hopes were dashed when the following morning and the one after that, Joan never showed.

Simon the Atheist

"Simon!" I heard a lady shouting from across the street. It was raining, hard, and this guy who was apparently called Simon, was leaving the local 76 gas station, heading towards nowhere in particular. The lady in the Ford Explorer who was calling after him, had been known to me for years. She lived full time in that vehicle, and before her current vehicle, a Ford Explorer, she'd lived in a VW Golf. That VW Golf was hilarious and really not fit for purpose. She'd drive into the 76-gas station every day at 5.30 am and then again at 2.30 pm, like clockwork, and as she touched the brake pedal to stop the car, all the lights around the car began to flash in sequence, just like a Christmas tree on wheels. On several occasions I'd asked the lady, (and even having spoken to her 5 or 6 times, I still didn't know her name), if she knew about her light situation, to which she'd reply "well, yes, it's my home and I don't want to sell it just yet, so I am very careful where and when I drive"

As if that made any difference, I thought.

This lady looked like a pencil, or a blonde version of Olive Oil from the cartoon Popeye. She was about 5 feet tall, if that, and the skinniest person I had ever met in my life. She had money, even though she lived in her car, but always seemed to spend it on cigarettes and potato chips. She would purchase an LA Times newspaper daily, sit inside her car with all the windows closed tightly, smoking heavily, and reading her newspaper from cover to cover. Quite how she managed to survive by not to gassing herself or contracting several types of cancers was beyond me, but every day she repeated that very same routine. Locked inside a box filled with poison, mind blowing!

"Simon!" she shouted again. But Simon ignored her calls and just walked on, oblivious to whatever skinny lady wanted from him. As he was coming towards me, and I was walking towards him, I decided to intervene.

"Simon!" I said, as I looked at him straight in his face.

"Do I know you?" he asked.

Simon's breath stunk of alcohol, and even though I was at least 6 or 7 feet away from him, the stench knocked me flat.

"I don't know you, but she does" I said, pointing to the skinny lady in the white Ford at the 76-gas station.

"That bitch! Fuck her!" he shouted, and then he looked at me and shouted again, "and FUCK YOU!", after which he staggered on down Niguel Road towards PCH and the golf course. The skinny lady had given up on Simon and was now back inside her car, smoking, eating chips and reading the LA Times, not caring at all that Simon had ignored her. I, on the other hand, felt jilted, for no other reason than all I was trying to do was help. 'Oh well', I thought, 'move on', and I did. I continued my walk, knowing that this was just another typical day in the life of Alan Zoltie. Off I went, around Salt Creek trail, and back towards the beach. I was listening to a book on my iPhone, engrossed in whatever the subject matter might have been and looking at some golfers teeing off on the 12th hole at Monarch Beach Golf Club, when out of nowhere appeared Simon, standing right in front of me. I stopped, he stopped and without hesitation, I shouted," FUCK YOU SIMON!" at the top of my voice.

Simon stopped and looked at me, staggering back and forth on one leg like the drunk he was, unable to balance and so obviously in a state of no return. He was one glass short of becoming a carpet, flat out and rigid.

Slurring his words, Simon began to speak," how'd you know my name", he stuttered, as his mouth tried to keep up with his brain.

"What are you doing out here Simon? This is not a place to stop and drink and it's certainly not a place to sleep."

"Fuck off" was all he could muster, and as he spoke, he withdrew a miniature bottle of what looked like bourbon from his rear trouser pocket.

"Take it easy Simon, let's not get that bottle out on this trail, I wouldn't want you to get arrested for drinking while intoxicated" I pleaded.

"I'm not drunk" Simon said, as he fell backwards onto the grass verge, dropping his bottle onto the concrete path, where it smashed into tiny pieces.

Simon was out cold, no longer able to walk, talk or drink. The stench emanating from his presence was vile and it was obvious Simon hadn't cleaned himself in months, if not years. It was sad to watch and even worse to comprehend let alone inhale this scene of complete depravation. The question was, or should I say, MY question was, what to do about what I'd just witnessed?

On the one hand, I could just walk away, kick the debris from his smashed bourbon bottle off the concrete path and into the grass to make sure no one passing in the hours to come would hurt themselves, or I could call the cops and have Simon taken away, or I could try and revive him, which was something I didn't quite feel like I could handle, bearing in mind the stench that emanated from his personage.

"Where's my bottle" Simon spoke!

Surprised by his ability to recover so quickly, I simply walked over to him and told him bluntly, "God took it from you before you could consume it, and God has sent you a sign that enough is enough."

"Fuck you" Simon spat while he laid flat on his back, his eyes staring up at my smiling face, "and fuck God. God doesn't exist, I can tell you that for a fact." He seemed adamant.

While he lay flat on the grass, while the stench from his body polluted the fresh morning air, and while birds sang all around him, Simon's demons were about to be released upon poor old me. The rant began, a drunken rant, but a rant all the same.

"You fucking piece of shit. You cock-sucker, motherfucking piece of shit. Where's my bottle, where's my fucking bottle?" I knew it was time to leave, as Simon's rage grew more intense by the second and even though I knew I could outrun him, if it came to a sprint and my requirement for a safe getaway, I didn't think it was worth talking the chance that Simon might possess hidden powers and find a way to catch me up and do some harm to my personage that I might end up regretting.

I was off, and as I walked away from Simon towards the beach, all I could hear were slanderous remarks and curse words following me through the still morning air.

At no point in time was I really afraid for my own safety, but with drunks, you never know what to expect and as I came around the corner of that trail, after passing under a tunnel, the sight of Salt Creek beach made for a welcome respite and a complete change of direction from Simon and his diabolical circumstances.

Bonnie The Buddhist

Skinny and dirty, although not filthy, she was attempting to mount her bicycle and quite frankly, she wasn't doing a very good job. It was 5.15 am on a very calm and cloudy July 4th morning, Independence Day 2023, and no one, I mean no one, other than the coyotes and the bunnies was on the trail. To see this lady attempting to get on a bike from a distance was disconcerting, only from the point of view that she was doing a lousy job and having great difficulty balancing on it. I approached her with a huge smile on my face, as I did with every person I came across on this trail, and as I got closer I realized that she was possibly homeless. Having made that determination and knowing from experience that homeless people can be erratic, I backed off slightly and decided I should be more cautious in what I was about to do and say.

"How's it going?" I asked her.

She smiled, and I could tell immediately she was either high or drunk. "I hope you don't mind me asking you," she said, in a very quiet unassuming manner, "but would you mind telling me what day it is? I know it's a crazy question, but I really need to know."

"July 4th" I said.

"Oh, really? And what day of the week is it?"

"Tuesday."

"Wow, thank you."

"Are you OK?" I asked her.

She smiled again and said, "Yes, I just need a lobotomy and a good 8 hours sleep."

'WTF!', I thought.

"Are you homeless? What's your name?"

"Yes, I am," she replied, and then continued, "I am Bonnie."

"Where are you from and where are you going Bonnie?" "I am from Arizona and I cycled here, so I am having, what you would call, a kind of run around, and when I am done, I will figure out what I want to do."

"So, you need medical assistance?" I persisted with my questioning, feeling very sorry for this poor soul.

"My uterus is falling out, and I haven't slept for over a week, and I really don't know what to do."

This explained her hesitation on getting back up on her bike. She looked like she was in agony.

"There's a hospital just down the street Bonnie, would you like me to give you directions? They have people there who can help you."

"No, I am a Buddhist, I can only be helped by people who understand my religion."

"I don't mean to sound ignorant Bonnie, but I'm sure the hospital will know exactly what you need and I'm positive they'll help in any way they can. If you're in pain you should go there now."

"July 4th?" she said.

"Yep, July 4th" I replied. And with that, she finally mounted her bike and rode off up the trail away from me and away from the hospital I had recommended.

I walked on, continued to listen to my book and not in the least concerned that Bonnie hadn't taken my advice, after all, I would never see her again, and she wasn't my problem. The beach came into view and after walking another 2.5 miles on the sand, something I always tried to finish each daily walk with, I climbed up a short steep hill and back onto the grassy trail that led up to my car in the parking lot. As I got to the top of the hill, Bonnie came rushing past me, cycling at the speed of sound, dark hair flowing behind her as the bike she was riding darted in and out of the bunny rabbits who were the only obstacles between her and Tour De France stardom. Obviously, she'd managed to make a remarkable recovery and was now truly mobile again. As she swished by me, I could hear her 'chanting' as if she were in prayer at the temple. It was loud and so obvious, and as she barreled down that path towards the end of the road, suddenly she applied her brakes to slow her down to a dead stop as a bunny ran right out in front of her. As I watched closely, Bonnie got off her bike and lay it on the path while she tried haplessly to chase that bunny all over the grass looking like she wanted to catch it. Such a bizarre scene, and with Bonnie having no chance against this athletic and speedy bunny, I looked on with laughter in my belly as this 'high' unwell Buddhist made several attempts to catch the rabbit, though for what reason I would never find out. Obviously, her uterus wasn't about to fall out, and maybe, just maybe, although I had my doubts, she wasn't actually homeless?

"Just another interesting day and another interesting walk in Dana Point." I thought, as I shrugged my shoulders and headed home.

The Cult

When I leave my home at 4 am or earlier each day, yes, 4 am and often 3.30 am, something I've done since Covid hit and the local gym closed, I rarely, if ever, give thought to the possible downside of walking 10 miles in pitch darkness on streets where very few normal people are to be found at that time of day. Until dawn breaks, which, depending on the time of year, can be 5 am or 7 am, people who roam our streets at that ungodly hour, can often be dubious characters, although obviously not in all cases. I have to admit though, I have seen some pretty scary stuff in the 4 years or so since these walks began to take priority in my fitness regimen. I have also seen things that have been majestic, magnificent and sometimes very unusual. Owls floating silently in and out of trees, dolphins jumping and playing games between themselves in the cool waters of the Pacific Ocean, coyotes, who will come right up to me and then cower like frightened dogs, into the bushes until I pass them by, shooting stars, streaking at the speed of light across darkened skies, magnificent sun-rises and amazing full moons, which illuminate the darkness of the ocean. What never ceases to amaze me though are the characters who frequent that time of day, or some might say, night. There's so much going on in the wee early hours, some good and some bad, but often what you will see or find is so contrary to anything one might conceivably call normal. People write stories and even books about these kinds of events, and although I am prepared for virtually anything, so much has happened to me which I believed could only happen to someone else. The sort of things you read about in the newspapers or watch on the 5 pm nightly news.

Four women, with their hands above their heads, placed on the top of a brand-new Tesla, surrounded by police, legs spread and about to be handcuffed.

It's a Tuesday morning, 4.35 am and it's all about to kick-off down at the Strands Beach parking lot.

I was walking towards this 'melee' with my air pods playing one of my audio books and drowning out all noise other than the narrators voice, when suddenly my eyes were distracted by flashing police-car lights 200 yards in front of me. They were mesmerizing in a kind of curious hypnotic way. It looked more like a disco in full swing, but without loud music and certainly no dancing. An eerie silence engulfed this chaotic scene and as I walked closer to the fracas, I casually but deliberately turned off my book, ready, and very willing, to listen in on whatever was about to go down. I'd just walked past a camper van which was parked on the side of the road adjacent to the parking lot, and as I did so, a light went on inside that van. Obviously, someone was living there, and he or she was probably homeless. There seemed to be quite a few vehicles on that street, which I walked past every two to three days, all containing people, homeless people, who were just living in their cars. I could tell by the blackout curtains on their car or van windows or the amount of junk they'd placed in the front seats, that someone/people were asleep in the rear seats, or that a family was having to bunk down for the night. From my experiences walking the streets of San Francisco for a week in 2006 as a homeless person, I learned that the average age for homelessness in the USA was 9 years old! Families who were unfortunate enough not to have homes, living rough, bringing their kids to safe residential areas just to sleep in the back of their car/van, then getting them ready and dressed for school in public restrooms, often filthy dirty restrooms, prepared to live like this for the sake of their kids, with little hope of seeing anything change and even less hope of watching their children grow up in a normal family environment. They had jobs, the kids had school, but neither added up to all of them having a home, a solid, permanent, reliable, comfortable home, something most of us just take for granted.

As I moved closer to this Tesla Model S, the four women now clearly visible to me, had their hands up and all of them seemed ready to be cuffed by the 6 local cops who'd surrounded them. Police radios were constantly chattering and breaking any normal early morning residential silence. I could always hear the chatter of birds and other wildlife at this particular hour, but the short sharp staccato bursts from police radios, made this day rather different from most and certainly quite interesting.

Barking orders at the women, all four were asked to place their hands behind their backs, and in unison, they obliged. I was just about at the vehicle and although unable and unwilling to stop and watch, I pretended everything was cool and that I was just another early riser out for a walk. One of the cops recognized me, (I'll explain why later in this book), and wished me a good morning. With a nod of my head, I acknowledged him, making sure to move on without causing any fuss while his colleagues did their jobs. One of the cops, a woman, was standing just behind the other 5, ready and willing to take care of the 'pat down' which was about to follow, when suddenly, from the van I'd passed where the light had gone on, a man jumped out of a sliding side door on the passenger side, waiving a gun high into the early morning darkness and cussing loudly into the still air.

"You fuckers all go to Hell! It's 4 am for fuck's sake. Get the Hell out of here. Don't you know people are trying to sleep?"

I stopped dead in my tracks, looking back towards this lunatic. The four women, who were about to be handcuffed, did the same. The cops however, took a different tact. I presumed, and it turned out I was completely wrong, they would crouch down and draw their guns and tell the guy to "drop it", just as you see in the movies, but instead, one of the officers looked at the guy and quite calmly said to him,

"Willy, get back in your van and go to sleep."

'WTF???' I thought, as I ducked to avoid what I believed would be a gunfight. Willy, the armed assailant, looked at the cop, put the gun down by his side and shouted again, 'fucking cops, go arrest a real criminal." At that point, the four women and the cops just started laughing. The guy had a gun, so if he wasn't a criminal, who was? One of the women, who had gone from crossing herself, (like the good Catholic she must have been), when the gun appeared, to laughing her head off when the cop so nonchalantly ordered Willy back into his van, blurted out, "you know him then?", directing her humor to no one in particular. I was stopped dead, unable to break away from this comedy show, although I use the word 'comedy' with the most flippant of it's meaning. I was actually shitting my own pants, thinking this could be my last moments on the planet.

The cops spoke, "Oh yes, that's Willy, and he's bi-polar. That gun he's brandishing is fake and we run across him all the time. He often comes out of that van threatening the locals, and we are called to come and sort out his mess quite frequently. He's totally harmless though."

"Jesus H" I thought, the guy had a gun and if the cops weren't on hand to reassure me and the four ladies, God only knows what would have happened. I made a mental note, change route and avoid Strands parking lot until it got light. The ladies were taken away, I never knew what their crime was, and Willy aimlessly sauntered back inside his van where he went back to sleep, I hoped! My walk continued, in an uneventful manner, thank goodness, but that incident kept me on edge for weeks and each time I passed Willy's van, I made sure to be as far away as that path would take me, in order not to encounter that nutjob again.

But Willy turned out to be the tip of the iceberg and one cog in the wheel of the 'Cult' I was about to encounter, made up of bi-polar, drunken, drug-infested, human beings, led by Willy and his right-hand man, Rob. It would change the way I looked at homeless people for a very long time to come. They were all part of this underground group, willing and desirous of living on the street and of creating as much grief as was humanly possible to anyone and everyone they could torment, something they managed to do with ease and with pleasure. Anarchists!

Gunslinging Willy and one-arm, Rob, two absolutely vile human beings. Willy, cut from the same cloth as Al, Capone, although that might be doing Al and injustice, and Rob, living rough on the streets since he was 17, now just about to turn 62. Both living in Willy's van and both willing and able to cause absolute chaos when needed. These two morons seem to control the local drug scene and many times, when passing Willy's van, deals were been done in front of my very eyes, with Rob, his back up and seemingly his henchman too, all too willing and able to throw abuse at me, threatening to 'decapitate my gentiles', or to 'make heaven my instant port of call', while he waved Willy's gun all around the fresh air his being polluted. As the police had mentioned, the gun was fake, but several times when passing this van, knowing who and what was going on inside its cabin, my mind always flashed to the possibility that they may just have a gun that was real and one day just shoot at me. This never happened, and of course, I tried as much as I could to avoid this area at these crazy early hours, but quite often, my bravado got the better of me and I just took a chance and walked right past them, finding that more often than not, they were both sleeping. Willy and Rob were always spouting crap about our government and how they were going to overthrow the President with their own gang, by using violent means to recapture America. I saw them once or twice with a few other 'anarchists' make threats to passers-by, unpleasant threats and threats that I believed should be taken seriously, but as I got to know a few of the local police, they assured me that Willy and Rob were pure bluster and should be laughed at as much as possible. I wonder if the cops felt the same about Lee Harvey Oswald? The gangs of vicious homeless men who seemed to gravitate occasionally to this van, made me question my own compassion for the homeless community. These people were unlike any homeless people I'd met in the past, all with one thing in common, to cause trouble. On a couple of occasions, I had actually stopped and spoken to Willy, one on one, only to be interrupted by Rob or another of the 'cult' they seemed to control, before Willy could have a proper conversation with me. These people came out of nowhere, and as soon as they did, I knew my time was up and I had to move along without bidding Willy goodbye. He and Rob were extremely controlling and I could tell by the way they spoke to the others who showed up now and again, who was boss. Willy's van is no longer parked at the same place it used to be, and I have no idea where he is now, but from the experience I had over a couple of years of seeing this mob, David Koresh seemed like a saint in comparison.

Yes, 4 am in the morning turned out to be a very interesting time of day, and one that got even more interesting one morning when, coming down the trail alongside Monarch Bay Golf club, I arrived at the tunnel which had been built to circumvent the need to cross PCH. I had walked through this tunnel hundreds of times prior to this particular morning, and the only issue I had ever encountered were those annoying teens on their electric bikes, you know the one's? They thrash their bikes at full throttle down that trail doing over 30MPH, don't give a hoot about anyone or anything in their path and when shouted at to slow down by passers bye, are never short of chutzpah in giving anyone who messes with their mojo the middle finger and a torrent of expletives in return. Bastards! Thank goodness these idiots are not around at 4am! One day someone in authority will need to take this issue of these kids and their new found toys and sort it out to the mutual satisfaction of all who share that rail and all the other trails in the area.

Inside the tunnel, I could see a body, sprawled out and lying on the sidewalk which ran the length of that tunnel and which was normally my sanctuary path, allowing me to avoid those teen idiots on their EB's when I took my second walk in the afternoons.

As I moved in closer, prepared as always to start a conversation with this new homeless obstacle, I noticed the many needles that surrounded his, so obviously still, body. This, I thought, might be a problem. I took out my phone, turned off the book I was listening to and approached the body with caution. Each step I took towards this stillness, each breath as my heart began pounding, each moment that passed as I came to the realization there was probably no life left in this bundle that was once human, brought bile and vomit from within my stomach all the way into my throat and it took everything I had inside my soul to prevent that bile from being ejected onto the sidewalk. The man was dead. His greying lifeless body, rigid and oblivious to my voice of concern and my gentle prodding of his face and stomach. He was stone cold and probably overdosed. Self-inflicted death, all too common on streets that have become so uncaring. I dialed 911 and said a prayer, a Jewish prayer, Kaddish.

It may have been too late for this young man, and yes, he was young, probably mid-twenties at most, but for all the others out there, the other cult members, ready and waiting to sacrifice their lives, just as this kid has sacrificed his, there lay only hope, however slim, however minimal, but hope nonetheless. My mission, to disband this cult, to pull whoever I could from its fiery grip, to educate, revive and revamp each and every one of those who, at this point in time, were nothing but lost souls, lost to the evils of drugs, alcohol and any other addiction, so rife, so prevalent and all too common on the streets of most major cities around the globe. This dead body I'd found represented so much that was so wrong in today's society and although this young man who lay lifeless in front of me didn't know it at the time, I was determined to make sure that his life would not be as worthless as his own self-belief had been and that for all those who found themselves in a similar position, all who were addicted, and about to become lifeless like him, I would champion for change, advocate for education and do my darndest to eradicate this vile disease from our society, if it was the last thing I did in life. I shed a tear, waited for the cops and moved on.

Mira The Evangelical

8 am, and breakfast was being served at RJ's by the Dana Point marina. They open at 6 and often by 8 you cannot get in the door for the throngs waiting outside to get a table, especially at weekends. A popular spot for sure, and a spot I, myself, although not enamored with, had frequented once or twice in the past. I walked past it now and again, enjoying the aroma of fresh cooked food which wafted gently into the harbor as I strolled by, enticing me, and many others, to enter and feast. The restaurant has its main entrance at the side of the building in a kind of strip mall, where guests can register for a table and then sit down, either inside or out, to enjoy their meals. They also had a rear entrance, which was basically on the main road where I usually walked, for staff and deliveries. And it was at that back entrance where I had the pleasure of meeting Mira.

Climbing out of a dumpster bin, she was sweaty, dirty, and very angry. Her long dark hair was tangled, having been left unwashed for months and her clothes looked like she was returning from a day down a coal mine. Her face was covered in blisters and her mouth was parched from lack of proper hydration. She walked with a limp and although I wasn't sure if that limp had materialized as she'd exited the dumpster bin, (it was very pronounced), her whole body shook and trembled with each step she attempted to make. Her speech, vile and distinct, was loud and very abusive, although she spoke to no one in particular and was seemingly mouthing off to the Gods.

"Fucking miserable, fucking stupid, fucking rich, fucking stop!" were just some of the incomplete sentences Mira was spouting into the, not so fresh, air.

Never one to shirk a challenge, or indeed a one on one with a homeless person, I shouted back,

"Yo! What's wrong with you? Can't you see people are trying to walk in peace here?" I said, smiling while staring her down in a friendly kind of manner.

Mira looked around, and then repeated that very same movement just to make sure she was looking in the right direction and that the words had come from my mouth and no one else's. She was clearly confused, and I could tell by her face that she wasn't sure if it had been me. There was no one else around and she soon figured out that her nemesis was indeed, the one and only.

"Who the fuck do you think you are? Billy Graham?" she shouted.

"I am anyone you want me to be." I replied.

"Well, Billy Graham saved my soul, so are you going to do the same?"

I looked her up and down, and I asked her with a straight face, "And which part of your soul did he save, because from where I'm standing, it doesn't look like he did a good job." I smiled, then continued, "find anything good in that dumpster?"

"Why do you care? Billy is the only man I ever met who cared."

"I see Billy left you with a lot to care about?"

"Fuck you!" she spat.

"No, FUCK YOU!" I shouted back. Mira was about 20 feet from where I stood and I knew from past experience that this encounter could now go either one of two ways. Mira would either laugh and start a slanging match, then calm down and chat, or, she would limp on down the road cursing me out and threatening me with untold violence.

"Well, Billy tried hard, and I just didn't listen" Mira said.

"Trying isn't the same as doing. How much did you give to him?" I asked. By now I could tell that Mira and I were going to have a conversation, if only for a few minutes, and she had no intentions of trying to do me any bodily harm.

"Too much" she said, as her face turned into a sulking representation of the thousands of dollars she'd parted with in the name of evangelical salvation. So typical of the USA. People taken in by so-called preachers and or saviors, all in the name of religion, redemption and salvation. While normal people gave and became poorer, most of these preachers/TV evangelists, got richer, caring little for anything or anyone outside of their crooked inner circle, destined to live their lives on private jets, 5-star hotel rooms and their 15 minutes or more of fame in a limelight that became a spotlight and a way of life paid for by others.

"You look hungry. Would you like food?" I asked.

"Yes, can you get me some?"

"I can get you most things as long as you are polite and grateful and tell me your name"

"Mira."

"Mira, I am Alan."

"Why are you talking to me Alan?" she asked, while frowning and pondering my motive.

"Mira, I talk to anyone and you look like you needed a friend, so here I am."

"Can you please get me coffee too?"

"Sure, I can get you all sorts of goodies, just wait here and stay out of the dumpsters."

Mira nodded, sat down on the curb and looked up towards heaven, saying a quick prayer and at the very end of that prayer, I could hear my name being spoken. I was touched.

Walking into RJ's, I ordered a full breakfast, scrambled eggs, sausage, bacon, hash browns and coffee to go. After paying, I walked back out to make sure Mira hadn't done a runner, and seeing she was still there, I decided she was definitely in for the long haul. I walked back into the restaurant and waited for my food to be made. Ten minutes went by, and the waitress came over to me with a plastic bag filled and brimming with food napkins and utensils. I picked up the bag in one hand, Mira's coffee in my other hand, and exited back out to the main road where Mira was waiting patiently.

"Let's walk across to the benches at the harbor" I suggested.

Mira agreed with a positive nod of her head and pulled herself up slowly from her sitting position to a standing angle, her limp didn't allow her to stand up straight, and she was obviously encouraged by the meal that she was ogling inside my plastic bag, convinced she was about to devour and enjoy it.

We sat, I opened the bag and took out a very warm polystyrene box, then plastic knives and forks and napkins and by this time her salivation was in full swing. Mira agreed that this was going to be a great day as she picked her way through a mountain of hash browns, topping up every mouthful with scrambled eggs and a little bacon here and there. She was in her element and her smile, probably a smile not seen in many years, beamed right across Dana Point Marina like a beacon, passing off a distinctive glow that no passerby could possibly ignore.

"Billy robbed me blind" she began, "but I was also stupid and gullible. He asked and I gave."

"Billy Graham?" I inquired.

"Of course, Billy Graham" Mira scolded me, suggesting I hadn't been paying attention. "Isn't that who we were talking about? He was on TV and I loved him. So charismatic. I used to drool when he'd come on and preach for an hour or more, taking in every word, every syllable, and when he was done and that 800 number appeared on the screen for me call and to pledge a donation, I was first in line, ready and willing to be saved with each dollar I promised."

"How much do you think you gave to his cause?"

"Thousands" she replied, as she put the last of the sausage into her mouth and began chewing, savoring every single morsel until it had gone.

"Where are you from?" I asked her.

"Oh, around here, but anyone who used to know me would never admit to that now, now that I live rough on these streets" she said, raising her head after sipping her scalding hot coffee and looking out into the distance as if she was remembering her past again. Obviously, from the look on her face, it probably seemed like a dream, which in turn had become a nightmare, leaving her stranded as a homeless statistic, and a person to be avoided.

"Mira, how'd you become homeless?" I asked, while being careful not to overstep any boundaries she might have had. As I knew so well, homeless people tended to be either extremely forthcoming when it came to discussing their prior lives, or they would clam up, say nothing and walk away. There was rarely a middle ground.

"Husband died, and he left me with a fortune in medical bills, which, I could never afford to pay and which the insurance company refused to cover and the hospital refused to forgive. One thing led to another, and, well, here I am. I lost everything"

A typical homeless story, I thought, and one I had heard so often in these past years of speaking with people just like Mira. No forgiveness from anyone in corporate America and a slippery slope for the innocent, leading to bankruptcy and then homelessness. This scenario was repeated almost every day in the United States of America. The richest country on the planet, unable and unwilling to help its own citizens out of a hole, whilst sending billions to countries who were run by dictators or tin pot governments and countries where those very same billions were instantly squandered or used for self-gain by leaders who were only interested in themselves and rarely interested in distribution to causes that the money was originally sent to assist. With the current situation of millions crossing our southern borders also draining the nations coffers, these handouts to countries and illegals were really a damning indictment of how fucked up the United States had become.

"I had a great home, a loving husband and we wanted to have kids," Mira was still talking, "but then James got sick, so sick that they fired him from his job, and well, he never made it, and in the end, neither did I. And now I think of all the money I gave to Billy, how I helped him, but when I went to my church for help, also Evangelicals, no one seemed to care. Not one person. Makes me sick to remember how I was treated. And here I am, and here I shall forever remain, homeless and a complete pariah."

I was about to speak, when Mira just stood up, looked at me for about half a second, never said another word, and walked away. My audience had come to an abrupt end, and I never knew if I would see that woman again. I threw her trash into one of the cans that dotted the parking lot, and walked the 4 miles back to my car, very upset at what was happening in America, and knowing that what I was uncovering was really the very tip of a huge iceberg that would probably never melt.

Part 2

The Congregation

There's no doubt that our streets have become more crowded and more violent over the past few years, with homelessness increasing and drug abuse out of control and all the programs required to rehabilitate just vanishing as government funding for those programs dissipates in favor of ridiculous schemes advocated by lobbyists and paid for with dollars that could be better used attending to our 'out of control' social issues, which only seem to be worsening as each day passes. These budget cuts have only served to increase a mostly unwilling congregation, all gathering in streets which hold little hope and even less chance of salvation. The churches of God are emptying slowly from lack of belief and the streets of Hell are filling rapidly, offering no chance for salvation. There's a seemingly unlimited number who belong to this congregation of Hell, some by choice, some by circumstance, but at the end of the day, whichever route has taken them there, it's a one-way ticket with very little chance of return.

In Portland Oregon, where the 26 meets the 405 and there's an exit to Portland city center, where a grass verge appears in my car window. I am driving, not too quickly, due to the traffic congestion synonymous for this part of town, when it just appears. Where all these freeways and city roads crisscross and where thousands of cars pass by each day, right bang in the center of this chaos, on that grassy verge, a congregation of tents are placed haphazardly amongst a backdrop of wealth and what used to be prosperous downtown Portland.

Amazed, but yet inwardly ashamed, I get off the freeway and park my car. I am ready and willing to investigate this unfortunate situation further. Walking up towards that tented city, my first notion was how difficult it must have been to navigate these busy roads to find this deserted space to live. After all, it had obviously been deserted for a reason? Inaccessibility, danger and noise, but three of the obvious traits that came to mind as I crossed over from one side of SW 13th Ave, under the 405 freeway and then up onto the grassy bank which housed about 60 homeless souls. Needles, trash of all kinds and discarded rotting sewage littered my pathway up that verge making me more nauseous with each careful step I took. Feeling my heart beat faster and faster, although not from the less than strenuous climb I was making, I was sure that if anyone was genuinely homeless, from experience, my safety was not really at risk. One never knew for sure, and as I came closer to 4 guys who were setting up what looked like the beginnings of a fire, my anxiety took over and my decision to venture into this encampment was being prejudged as good and bad by the left and right side of my brain. Oh, how I longed for company or back up, but it was too late and person A was walking quickly towards me with a look of disgust on his face. I was about to be confronted by an Islamic homeless commune who had claimed this patch of grass as their own, although at that point in time, I had no idea who they really were.

"As-salamu-alaikum" the man said, as he came closer to where I'd stopped.

"Wa-alaikum-salam" I replied.

I had spent much time in Israel during my many years of traveling this earth and at one point in time, when I worked on a Kibbutz for 6 months, had picked up several Arabic words and customs. I had also learned the standard greeting, which the two of us has just performed, and which seemed to place the man, who now stood before me, completely at ease.

I decided to let him speak first, just to gauge the tone of his mood and figure out the possibility of their cooperation or contribution towards my book.

In a broad Texas drawl, the man continued, "Are you lost my friend?"

I smiled. "No, I was passing by, driving to the airport and I saw you guys camped out on this patch of grass. I've been working with homeless people for many years, and I'm presuming that you are all homeless right now and unable to integrate into society?"

"What has that got to do with you?" he asked, and when he asked that question, I could tell he wasn't curious, but perhaps angry by my uninvited intrusion.

To diffuse his oncoming annoyance, I deflected by saying, "I am only here to offer help. I was homeless once and I try to give back to those less fortunate that myself, and if you're interested in assistance, however small, that I can offer today, I would love to chat with all of you for a few minutes. Hey, if we don't chat, how are we ever going to resolve this homeless crisis?"

He stood still and rigid and thought, and as he did this, he began to smile.

"You want to help us?" he laughed, "and exactly how are you able to do that?"

Three other guys were now standing next to him, and I suddenly felt way outnumbered and very uncomfortable.

"As you can tell from my accent, I am not from here. I have spent my life advocating for an end to this 'disease' called homelessness and I have written books, worked in shelters, walked these streets, trying to figure out how we can all work together to put roofs over the heads of people who are forced to live like you guys, out in the open and stuck between freeways, and to find a way forward, conversations between those who are and those who are not homeless, need to be had. I do my best to chat to as many homeless people as is humanly possible, no matter color, creed or religion, because the only way this issue is ever going to be resolved is if we all work as one and figure out a solution."

Man number 1, applauded my little speech, and man number 2 and 3 joined in.

"Yes," he said, "but what can you do for us?"

"Let's sit and chat for a few minutes and we can try to figure that out."

They all sat down on the grass and I joined them. More curious heads poked out of their pitched tent doors and before I could count to 5, there were at least 20 people sitting together in front of me as the conversations began.

"Are you all followers of Islam?" I asked the group.

"We are, although we have one or two who just joined us because they enjoy the view" number 1 said, as he laughed and looked around at the hundreds of cars whizzing past.

"Are you not welcomed at the local mosque?" I continued, "and don't they cater for your meals and other needs in there?"

Number 1 looked at me and laughed again, "yes, sometimes, but the nearest mosque is very far to walk and none of us have cars. We ended up here because most of the other homeless souls here in Portland didn't like the idea we were Muslims and so we were castigated and then banished by those who thought they were superior to us. We are very capable of surviving on our own, and with the help of Allah, we will all survive."

"You're from Texas? How'd you end up in Portland?" I asked.

"Allah brought me here, just like the others in this group. Some of us walked here, some drove and I came on a bus, but for whatever the reason, and only Allah knows, we are all here together. These people," and he pointed to 5 or 6 black people in the group, "came from Ethiopia, or Eretria, all refugees and all looking for work, but the rest of us are from the USA."

"And you are homeless because??"

"Because the United States of America doesn't care about its own people!"

number 1 declared in a loud voice, followed by a 'here, here!' uttered in unison by about half of the other people in the group.

"How do you survive out in this space?"

"We manage, and we manage well." He said, and it was at that point in time where I needed to make a decision on whether to press him on his leadership of this congregation or leave it alone and change subject matters. I went for it, ready to run if I had to, but hoping he's talk some more.

"So, you're the 'Imam' of this group?" I asked.

Number 1 had the looks of an Imam, wearing a white loose-fitting robe, Jesus sandals, and a beard that hung at least 12 to 15 inches off his chin. He looked reverential. He looked like he had been educated in the ways of Islam, but he also looked like he had a mean streak, which was so evident in his eyes and I figured that somewhere or other, this man was an ex-con, or ex-military, where Islam had been his mainstay while he'd served his time in either.

I was to be proven right once again, when Number 1 answered my pending question.

"You could say that, but I prefer to say we share those responsibilities"

Yeah, right, I thought, tell that to the 12 or 13 women who were sitting around looking like they were used and abused. They all had a look of 'I just don't want to be here, but have no choice in the matter'.

Number 1 asked again, "So, what are you going to do for us?"

The one thing I can say is that whatever it was I was about to offer, no matter how generous, it would never be enough. These people were stuck in the middle of a crises, a political mess and a local disaster. With tens of thousands, homeless in Portland and millions more in other cities, I knew and they knew, life wasn't about to change for the better. Yes, they might be offered some food now and again, and yes, money too, but in general, they were stuck, caught up in a miserable existence that had been created, in most cases, buy circumstances beyond their own control.

What do you guys need?" I asked, "I have limited time and limited resources and as I mentioned to you earlier, the only reason I stopped to look and try to talk to all of you was purely selfish from my standpoint, and I hadn't bargained for the 20 or so of you to be in such a mess!"

"You think this is a mess?" said Number 1, "we are living like kings compared to others we have spoken to."

"Yes, I am sure of that" I replied.

'What we are really in need of is housing, proper housing. We are not druggies and we are not alcoholics, we are devout Muslims, discarded by not only our own faith, but by other faiths too. There are not enough people out there trying to separate real and genuine homeless people from those who are anarchists and homeless by choice. We need help, yes, lots of help, but we need help from people who will believe in us, help us rebuild and give us back our self-respect."

I knew this was the hardest thing to give anyone in their situation. Self-respect was something to be earned though and not given, but self-respect cannot be earned until there's a platform to build from and right there and then, guaranteeing self-respect to a bunch of strangers I had just met, was way above my remit and pay grade. My abilities were indeed limited as were most people who popped by this camp to donate blankets and food and sometimes cash. We were all limited in what we could do, but nonetheless, people like me and people with more influence than I would ever have, tried constantly to make the lives of those on their streets, better, if only in small pieces.

Koran in hand, Number 1 retreated with a parting shot, as he and the others stood up and went back towards their tents,

"Thanks for stopping by, and when you can figure out how our lives can improve without us begging, please feel free to return."

As traffic on all freeways surrounding the camp came to a rush hour standstill, I took a last look at the condition these Muslims were living in, looked to the sky and asked Allah to help, even though I knew they were all doing that very same thing at the very same moment. At the end of the day, God, Allah, Buddha, and anyone else you care to mention, were never going to fix, what was certainly, an epidemic which was out of control. It would only be us, normal every day human beings who would be able to change this perverse, disgusting and on-going issue, an issue which was about to get worse and an issue which was about to get even more intolerable for those who found themselves stuck in a place without walls but with the invisible bars of one of the largest jail cells anyone could ever imagine.

Two blocks and about 30 homeless people later, I was back in my car and back on the road, this time, headed to Portland's famous waterfront. It was time to eat and time to figure out what, if anything I could do for those people I'd just left. Parking my car close to the River Place hotel, locking it, double checking that it was indeed locked, I walked around the corner towards a row of shops next to the hotel, where McCormick and Schmick seafood restaurant was situated. This restaurant had become one of my favorites since I started coming to Portland in the late 1990's. I used to stay in the River Place hotel on a regular basis and loved not only the location, but the service, the comfort and the view. Situated right on top of the Columbia River, there's so much going on and lots of interesting things to see and to do. I wrote in my last book, Poems from Cardboard City, about the guy I met just on the grass outside the hotel, who'd set up a mini golf course, using only sticks and branches from trees and an old tennis ball. He's built 9 hard looking holes and spent his days practicing like a pro, hopefully, and to the annoyance of most who were passing by, not to hit anyone with errant golf shots, something he tended to do with regularity.

Portland, as the sign says, has to be kept weird, and on this grass bank by the river, which stretched for at least 1.5 miles in both directions, were some of the strangest people I have even seen in my entire life. From all of those I had spoken to over the years, there was none stranger than Mad Meg, as I would call her, a 60 something homeless vet, half man/half woman, although it was never clarified to me in person, which half was which. Meg was, according to the three times I had met her, an outright proponent of the Occult. She was a wiccan, a witch, and a self-proclaimed wizard. Or maybe he was a wizard and the she half was a witch? Who knew? In any event, my task that evening was to locate Mad Meg, something I hadn't been able to do for several years due to Covid and various other reasons that had kept me away from Portland. Mad Meg though would remember me, assuming she was still alive, having spent one horribly cold evening with her in the winter of 2015, helping her fend off a bunch of local 'lefty' politicians, who were intent on destroying her little patch of sanity, her tent made from plastic sheeting, and kicking her off this one small patch of grass where she'd been living for more than 10 years previous to this unfortunate encounter. Mad Meg, was truly mad, though some sense could be made from the occasional conversations I'd had with her, if one could decipher the BS and illegible vocabulary that encapsulated most of what she was trying to tell me. She was synonymous for harassing locals and tourists alike. Verbally abusing all who stood in her way, with words that were as foreign to me as they were to the publishers of the Oxford English Dictionary. The night I met Meg, the very first night, it was around 5 pm, pitch black and freezing cold and about to start snowing. Mid-January, 2015 I believe, and I was out walking to the Pearl district, a lovely, although not so much now, part of Portland's downtown, filled with restaurants, shops and beautiful apartment buildings. I was running late, having parked at the River Place hotel, gone to my room, dropped off all my samples that I'd carried around all day for meetings at Nike's HQ in Beaverton, washed my face and decided that a taxi was just too luxurious a way to travel the measly 2.5 miles to the restaurant where I was meeting my friends for dinner. Walking would suffice and it would save on a taxi fare that I could donate to someone in need. It would also give me the chance to 'bed in' my new Nike sneakers I'd purchased in the employee store that very afternoon. Off I went, fearing little other than the cold wind which had begun to blow from the north. Moving at a swift pace, my sneakers feeling just great, I had walked about ¾ of a mile when this thing, yes, that's the only description I can give, a thing of absolute indescribable ugliness, standing by a huge oil drum, which was holding an everlasting bonfire to keep her/him warm, appeared out of nowhere.

The abuse was immediate and unrestrained.

"Hey" he/she, blurted," you fucking piece of cunty shit sliced vermin rich bastard."

I ignored the onslaught, believing this thing was just another of Portland's insane homeless community, harmless and mouthy, full of bluster with no intent to harm. This would be an apt description for most of the people who occupied the tents and cardboard boxes along Portland's once beautify streets, and although most were not as mouthy as Meg, their ability to insult and harass, was just as great.

This thing decided to stand right in front of my chosen path, and with little time or room to maneuver, it seemed a head-on confrontation would be the order of that moment.

"Fuck off, you slimeball cretin" I shouted back.

"I am ready to cast a spell on your sorry ass" it said.

"Go for it, and remember, I have superpowers, and any spell you cast will rebound and hit you right in your face, causing you nothing but misery and suffering for all eternity."

Sometimes I just didn't know where my one-line responses came from, but I had to laugh and admit, they were often good and very appropriate.

"Are you from another planet?" it asked.

"Yes, planet Scotland" I replied.

"How can you speak English?"

"I was trained on my planet from birth. I am here to rid this world of all vulgarity, and you are my first victim," I said, trying hard to move past this 'thing' and get to my dinner appointment.

"Well, I am a witch", she said. After hearing she was a witch, I was now convinced she was indeed a she. Remember these were the days before all this stupid and irrelevant pronoun association. (MY opinion, of course!) When asked nowadays what my pronouns are, I normally respond with Rich/Handsome or Fuck and You!

"Let me see you cast a spell" I told her, and as I said this, my walk came to an abrupt halt. I knew a conversation of some kind was about to take place between the 2 of us. Her hand was stuck in an upward position and before I could say Abracadabra, she produced a magic wand from underneath this blanket which was wrapped around her upper body keeping her warm. The wand was made of wood and looked like the cut off narrow end of a pool cue. Meg, spun the wand around in circles, at first clockwise and then in the opposite direction, muttering various words from underneath her steamy, and obviously drug-infused, breath. "What mumbo-jumbo is that you're talking?" I asked her, as politely as I could.

"Brighid, my love and my salvation." she replied. As if I would have any idea who or what that was.

"OK excellent, and how will this prayer cast a spell on me?"

"It will bring an end to winter and your life will be filled with sunshine" she replied.

"So far so good. That's a magical spell. I need more sunshine" I insisted.

"Everyone does" she said.

"And your name is??" I asked.

"Meg. Queen of Portland, savior of all the planet earth."

"Well, Meg, savior of planet earth, I need to get going, so let me know if I can buy you some food or drink, the soft kind, no alcohol"

"Please don't go" she insisted, "I have not finished my prayers yet and I still want to cast a spell on you."

"I will see you on the flip side Meg" I told her, as I began to walk once again in the direction of the restaurant where I was going to meet my buddies.

About two hours later, meal over, I was about to walk back to the hotel when one of the guys in our group offered me a ride to the hotel. I thought that would be a great idea since it was past 9 pm and the evil that is Portland's bad side begins to show its ugly face. Safer to drive, I thought, so I accepted and got into the front of Stan's car. Stan, my buddy, drove a Nissan Maxima, and had just had it cleaned. We took off towards the hotel and just as we approached 6th and Broadway, Meg jumped out of nowhere, with virtually no clothes on, right in front of Stan's car, waving her 'magic' wand, and shouting obscenities at anyone and everyone who would listen. "That's Meg" I told Stan.

"You know her??" he said.

"We're old friends" I replied, as I smiled and got out of the car to try and calm her down. She was cursing like a trooper, each word, delicately poised on the tip of her tongue to be shouted out with the utmost force and disgust. "Meg! Meg!" I shouted, as Stan stayed behind the wheel of his Nissan, pissing himself laughing, and so obviously intrigued by what was going down. He looked flabbergasted, and quite rightly so.

"Meg, get off the road and shut the fuck up!" I said, as I pulled her half-naked body from the center of that busy junction, and ushered her back onto the sidewalk.

"What the fuck do you think you are doing?"

"I'm a witch, I'm a witch" she shouted, as she danced around in circles, waving her wand as if it was about to fire bullets into the now, gathering crowd of interested onlookers.

"Meg, we all know you're a witch, but even witches can get killed by passing cars!"

"Witches don't die" she insisted.

"Then what happens to them?" I asked, while I attempted to get her out of the street.

"Witches come back again and again, and will be here through all eternity."

"Right, and you've been here many times before?" I said, sarcastically.

"I have, but not always here. I am a witch of many guises" she said with a very serious face.

"OK Meg, let's forget about the past and start thinking about this very moment. Where are you going and why are you trying to get yourself killed?"

"I will never die!" she said, defiantly.

"Meg, I can assure you, you will, and if you carry on thinking you won't, it'll happen sooner than you expect."

"Got any cash?" she asked, as she changed the subject.

"You in need of a new wand?"

"Very funny" she replied, "my spell on you will be extremely harsh" she promised.

"Not if you want cash, it won't" I said with some bravado.

She stopped and thought about that last comment and I could see the cogs in her brain spinning round and round trying to work out a response, all the while knowing she needed money and that money looked like it might come from my pocket. My buddy Stan was still patiently waiting in his car, pulled over to the side of the street, and laughing his head off as he watched in awe, this two-way banter back and forth, without commenting or suggesting there might eventually be a winner between Meg and me.

"OK," Meg said, "I'll do a deal with you. Give me $5, no, wait, make it $10, and I will make sure the spell I already put on you is dissolved and no harm will come to you."

"Hang on Meg, when we met a few hours ago, did you put a spell on me then?" I smiled and gave her a look filled with complete disbelief. She was a wise old owl and very street smart. As she tried to figure out yet another response, I removed $5 from my wallet and gave it to her.

"Meg, I need you to promise me you will not buy drugs with this money and that it will only be used to get yourself a new wand, or, at the very least, a Big Mac and some fries?

She took the money, looked me straight in the eyes and said, "FUCK YOU!", and then began reciting some gibberish that I couldn't understand and which seemed to be her spell. She waved her wand back and forth, mouthing words I had never heard before, pocketed the cash I'd given her, waved the wand one last time and then, just like her magic, she was gone, gone into the night, never to be seen again, well, not for a year or two.

Which brings me back to this particular evening, some years later.

As I walked along Portland's grassy river bank, that particular evening, after my conversation with the Muslims, Meg was the only thing on my mind and finding her, although not a priority, was something I intended to do, just to make sure she was still living her life, well into her guaranteed eternity.

Under the Morrison Street bridge, I could see a fire burning, not a huge fire, but a fire in an oil drum. The glow of the flames, lighting up what was a very dull and miserable evening, with clouds and the probability of rain looming on a blackened horizon. Portland, synonymous for its continual rainfall, (it gets more rain than Seattle, Google it), can be a four-season experience, in one day, and believe me, I have seen this several times. Rain, snow, sun and more, all in the space of hours, not months. This fire, inside the oil drum, was surrounded by at least 6 bodies, all trying to stay warm and dry, and all of whom were so obviously homeless. As I approached, with caution of course, my eyes and ears darting from side to side and back to front to assess any danger that may be lurking beyond the innocence of that fire and its purpose, I noticed Meg, but not the Meg I had met in the past. This version of Meg was thinner, dirtier, and certainly louder, (if that was possible), than the previous Meg, but this Meg still carried, what looked like, a brand-new wand. Gone was the old pool cue end, and in had come a crooked tree branch, about 18 inches long and thick at the bottom. Meg was in full flow, verbally assaulting any ear she could bend, caring little for the friends she would insult and determined to cast spells on anyone who claimed anything to do with her.

"Meg!" I shouted, interrupting her diatribe and causing consternation with the other 5 bodies who surrounded the oil drum.

"What!" she shouted back.

"Remember me?" I asked.

"No, who the fuck are you?" she snarled.

"I saved your life, and you don't remember me?"

"Fuck off or I'll cast a spell on you" she shouted.

"Got any spare cash?" one of the bodies asked.

"Yes, but only for Meg" I replied.

The other 5 bodies turned around and looked at me, wondering what the heck was going on. Meg stopped talking and pointed her wand directly at my person, and suddenly burst into song, I presumed another curse was coming my way, but this song seemed more mellow and kind of endearing.

"Why only for her?" another body asked.

"Because she placed a spell on me that anytime I came to Portland I would seek her out and give her $20" I lied.

"She did?" asked another.

"Yes, she did. Meg, can you remember me now?" I asked her.

"NO, now FUCK OFF, I am busy, and leave me the $20 before you go" she said, quite annoyed and so obviously confused.

One of the other bodies piped up.

"I'm a wizard" he said, with a straight face but with a wry smile hidden under that straightness.

"You are?" I laughed.

"Yes, and I am going to place a spell on you that every time you come to Portland you need to deliver $100 to me in person, or you will rot in Hell."

"My friend," I said, addressing him directly, "I am already burning in Hell just watching you and your homeless friends suffering every day in this purgatory. "Meg," I said, as I took the $20 from my back pocket, handing it over to her cautiously, "here's your $20, stay safe and keep away from trouble."

I walked on, listening to all of them argue about how to spend Meg's windfall, and with Meg, speaking louder than the others, telling each and every one of them that they would all be under her magical influence until the died a horrible death. I never found her again, even though I made several attempts, and to this day, I have no idea what happened to Meg, or if she even made it through all eternity as the 'not so' wicked witch of the west.

Drunk Dan

Vashon Island was discovered by a British Admiral George Vancouver in 1792, and named it after one of his captains, James Vashon. It sits about 5 miles to the west of Seattle International airport, right bang in the middle of the Puget Sound, and is home to about 7000 permanent residents and 3000 to 4000 transient residents, who come for weekends or just to spend their summer vacations in solitude and semi-remoteness.

In 2015, I, for various reasons, decided to move onto Vashon Island and set up home, thinking a little peace and quiet might be good for the soul and give me space and time to pursue the things which were important to me. I purchased a home and land, literally in the middle of nowhere, hoping that the commute by boat, the only way to get on or off Vashon, didn't drive me to drink before the remoteness of island life did. Settling in was fairly easy, although weather issues, having arrived from spending 20 years in sunny California, soon put a dampener, (pardon the pun), on expectations and an ability to come to terms with gloomy rainy weather patterns that could last for weeks. Vashon itself proved to be a very interesting and eclectic environment, filled and brimming with 'could've-would've' people and, if you don't know what that means, apologies.

My first impressions turned out to be my last impressions, when I left the island in 2020, and those impressions, which are still with me today, are of an amazing community trying hard to be compassionate to those who were the selected and unfortunate few. The churches on Vashon, and there were many, had a food program for people, who needed serious assistance to survive their daily grind, taking turns to make dinners for families, especially those with kids, on a nightly basis, with food prepared by locals and served by church members. I loved this program and helped out a few times by delivering food and solace to those who need it most. There were however, some who lived on the island, who were beyond hope and help.

Drunk Dan was one of those.

He approached the pharmacy looking like he'd been working down a coal mine for the past 10 years without ever washing or changing clothes. His oversized coat, dragging behind his unwashed body, and his hair and face, all matted and black from lack of care and attention. He was about 45, although he looked 70 and his complexation, well, let's just say, it was drug and alcohol infused. He had pot holes on his face, and a swagger that suggested he'd been on the booze for more than just one or two decades. It was the first time I'd had the pleasure of seeing Dan, and as it was my first week on Vashon, the fact that anyone could be homeless on an island, shocked me into a realization that poverty, mental health issues, alcoholism, drugs addiction and abuse, avoided no place on earth. It was sad to think that an island in the middle of nowhere in particular, contained people who had no place to live and no place to go. Dan, as I would find out later, actually lived in a tent in someone's garden, but that first encounter, left me confused and saddened that alcohol and drugs could turn any man or woman in any town on the planet, into a Dan.

Dan walked past me that morning, muttering something abusive under his breath as he decided to turn his nose up at me and, instead of giving me room to pass, made it clear, that HIS street would not be for sharing. Unfazed, I stared right back into his face, with my usual smile, making it clear to him, that I was not there to be intimidated. This scene would be repeated many times over the coming years that I lived on Vashon, and even though I never got to know Dan all that well, I had conversations with him that were quite enlightening. Dan kept up the same routine every day in his life. From Monday to Sunday, he showed up in the same places, muttering the same obscenities under his breath, looking for the same hand-outs, some which he received regularly, and some which he could only wish for, but nonetheless, this was his patch, and he was going nowhere. There is only one main street on Vashon which boasts stores and restaurants and not too many to boot. That street is about as long as most driveways on the island, so Dan really had on the one hand a captive audience, but on the other hand, always the same people day in and day out to bother and harass, other than when the tourists came, then his audience suddenly doubled. His hand-out influence was limited, to say the least, and once people got to know him, they avoided him like the plague. Dan would often go from store to store, hang around inside the store, not causing trouble, but looking directly at the staff and hoping for something, either a bite to eat, or cash. Dan was also often seen sitting on a bench in the middle of what would be the site for Vashon's weekend farmers market, smoking, drinking alcohol or just cursing at passersby. Dan was also schizophrenic, but I didn't know this until someone told me, which was about a year after my first encounter with him. My one and only serious conversation with Dan was about 3 years after I moved to Vashon. I was walking into the pharmacy to collect a prescription, and he was blocking, although not intentionally, the front entrance to the store. He seemed 'away with the fairies', as my mother used to say, and impossibly lost in his own thoughts, not realizing where he was or what he was doing.

"Excuse me Dan" I said, as I tried to push by him and enter the store.

"How'd you know my name?" he asked.

"Everyone knows your name Dan" I told him.

"Well how do YOU know it?" he asked again.

"Dan, can you please move out of the door way so I can get inside?" I asked politely. He stank, and the stench coming from him of unwashed flesh, clothes and alcohol abuse, was really overwhelming and vile.

"Dan, are you OK? Have you had anything to eat today?" I was curious.

His mood softened, but only for a brief moment.

"I need a drink and some cash" he said.

"Don't we all?" I replied.

"C'mon man, help me out" he begged.

"Dan, let me into the store and when I come out, we can chat"

He moved to one side and I entered.

Ten minutes later I exited, and Dan was nowhere to be seen. He's vanished into thin air, something almost impossible on an island, but something Dan was very good at. He had a habit of appearing from nowhere in particular and then vanishing, like the magician he clearly liked to be. One time in particular I was walking down the main road on Vashon with my friend and his grandkids, when, from behind this bush, and although not in full view of the public's eyes, clearly exposed, Dan shouted out, "mind the kids, I am taking a piss", as the stench of his steaming urine, wafted into a cold winter's afternoon air, polluting not only the plants he'd pissed on, but the memories of all who had the displeasure of experiencing his disgusting behavior. Yes, Dan was a character and he loved to play out his nuances in front of what he called, 'HIS CONGREGATION".

I found him again while I was walking back to my car that morning, only this time, he was pleading with an elderly lady to give him cash. I interrupted his appeal, simply by tapping him on the shoulder and saying,

"I thought we agreed that you'd wait for me outside the pharmacy?"

"Who are you?" he said, looking stunned and aggrieved at the same time. I'd broken up his little soliloquy to this, clearly frightened and annoyed elderly lady, and Dan, who now knew she wasn't donating to his cause, was frustrated and becoming angrier by the minute.

His scowl became his trademark. He tried to frighten anyone who dared look at him, but he rarely succeeded in doing anything other than make people laugh, if only in pity.

"Dan, let's chat?" I suggested.

I signaled for him to follow me and as we walked towards the local bakery, I thought about all the other homeless people I'd met over the years, all of whom probably had mental health issues of some sort, but none of whom had been as aloof or as affected by their issues as Dan seemed to be. He showed signs of a man in complete turmoil, both outwardly and inwardly, but also of someone who had been perhaps normal at some point in time, although I found it hard to make that scenario a reality in my own mind. People who I'd spoken to who'd lived on Vashon for many years, often ridiculed Dan or fobbed him off as just another nutcase, while sometimes recounting stories of him when he had a little more sanity. Although to be honest, the sanity they referred to, was, in my humble opinion, grasping at straws and a thing of Dan's distant past. The only thing that seemed sane to me about Dan at that point in time was his consistency. He always seemed to be in the same places at the same times and on the same days. Perhaps that was my imagination playing tricks with desire to chat with him, or perhaps it was just Dan being Dan. I was about to find out.

"These people are my congregation" he said.

"What do you mean?" I asked him, having no idea what he was talking about.

He then went off on a tangent.

Bearing in mind Dan looked like he'd jumped out of a dumpster, all the time, and bearing in mind he stunk to high heaven, his next statement rocked me in my boots.

"The only thing is, I need to be very selective with the girls I date" he said.

"WTF???" I said, "you date?"

"Oh yes, but only Christians" he replied.

"Why's that?" I persisted.

"I think after I finish being sober, and you know, it's been 72 days since I had a drink, I'll go and get a proper job!" he smiled.

"What kind of job?" I asked.

Knowing he'd never done a day's work in his life, I was intrigued.

"I think I will weed whack or mow lawns." he said, triumphantly.

I knew for a fact that Dan had once swept the floors at Vashon's famous pizza joint, The Rock, and had been fired for his inactivity and inability to perform manual work, so my next question was fairly obvious.

"You up for the task Dan? You think you can work that hard?"

"Piece of piss" he said, "I can do anything I want."

While drunk perhaps, but not sober and the only thing I figured he could do comfortably was to fall down and get up again, once every 3 or 4 hours, in between the drink and the drugs.

"So" I said, "tell me about your congregation?"

"They love me here, and I love them all. I get fed, I sometimes get drink, drugs are easy and they all pray for my soul, or so they say."

"Very cool."

"Now," he asked, "what are you going to get for me?"

"What would you like?"

"Beers."

As he said that, he emphasized the S at the end of beer.

"I'll tell you what. I will get you a slice of pizza. How does that sound?"

"C'mon man!" he said, his eyes pleading for more.

"That's the final offer, take it or leave it."

"Fuck you!" and as he said this, his scowl returned, with Dan trying to look as intimidating as was humanly possible. He didn't succeed, and my next question just destroyed him.

"What would all these good Christians in your congregation think if they knew you were turning down free pizza from a good Samaritan like me?"

He was speechless, and walked away, giving me the middle finger as he did so. Dan and I never spoke again, indeed, after our conversation that day, every time I saw him, he ignored me completely. The fact is, I just don't think he remembered who I was, and he'd moved on to the next member of the community in the hope that beers with and S would be more forthcoming from a decent Christian, not a fake like me!

The Pulpit

I once wrote a poem, The Prayer, (it's on my web site, alanzoltie.com), where I had a conversation with God. Albeit brief, the conversation was certainly sincere, and when I passed on that poem to my friend Paul in London, he was enamored enough that he sent it to his priest, who in turn read it out to his congregation that Sunday, who in turn passed it on to their friends and families, who then made the poem a smash hit amongst the Catholic community in the UK. A simple poem, written by a Jew, read out by a Catholic, then revered by Christians. Amazing how small the world can get, I thought, and if that's the case by writing a few words and commanding such enormous respect, what would happen if I wrote a book, which I eventually did, outlining how severe our homeless crises is and how undignified those who are stuck in this vicious circle must feel? Religion, it seemed at the time, was so unimportant if you found yourself homeless, yet, when digging deeper into the homeless crises, I noticed that religion certainly played a huge part in how homeless people spent their time and their energy, rarely loosing hope or faith in their Gods. Self-esteem, as outlined in my last book, Cardboard City, makes all the difference and as you have seen from the preceding pages, give someone who has nothing just a little something and that little something can change a life. I am not saying I have the cure for homelessness, and this book isn't about changing anyone's opinion on how we should cure this crisis, but a little goes a long way, and respect goes even further. Some of the people I have met in my 40 odd years of dealing with homeless people do not deserve respect, in fact, some of these people do not deserve anything more than a good kick up their backsides and a simple question, asked to their faces, "why are you here when you can live a normal life without handouts?"

One man in particular who comes to mind, and I call him a man, but honestly, the guy I am about to reveal needed to grow a pair, and all will become clear as you read on.

Harry is a pimp, not a pimp in the sexual sense, but a pimp all the same. After all, a pimp is a pimp is a pimp, and all pimps require is control of their prey and financial gain from those they control. Money and respect, governed by rules and fear.

Harry, also known as Hamza, which is his real Russian name, came to America in 2004. His family, all Russian Orthodox Christians, fled to California to avoid what they believed was going to be an overly oppressive government, led by Putin, and boy, were they right. Harry was 15 at that time and the family, as I said before, all God-fearing people, ended up in Los Angeles, specifically Santa Monica, where Harry went to school and his father worked 3 jobs to keep the family alive and well. At first Harry, led in part by the encouragement of his older sister, continued his religious studies and beliefs at a Russian Orthodox church in Hollywood Hills, where he and his family would attend services on a regular basis. Harry however, attending a regular public school close to where the family lived in Santa Monica, would soon have his head turned by 'so-called' friends he made, who then influenced, not only his introvert behavioral patterns, but his beliefs too.

Harry became a problem for his parents, experimenting in drugs, sex, both with girls and boys, and he began stealing. At first the thefts were small, cigarettes and chocolate from his local

7-Eleven, then progressing to bikes and cars, which then led to his first brush with the law. Harry was 17 years old when the cops showed up on his parents' doorstep with an arrest warrant for grand theft auto.

From that day onwards, Harry's life spiraled out of control, and not in a good way.

It was summer of 2018, and I was up in Santa Monica to meet my friend Gavin for lunch. We were meeting at the Old Kings Head pub, my choice, and I was early. Parking the car had not been easy, and having driven around the block several times without any success in finding a spot, I was stopped at a red light waiting to turn right, when suddenly out of nowhere this drunk woman, armed with a sponge and cloth, pounced on my stationary car and began washing the windshield. My cars are always spotless and her interference with dirty soapy water on my sparklingly clean windshield, was something I just didn't need.

"Ge the fuck off my car!!" I screamed through the window, hoping she'd take heed and stop what she was doing. Too late, the water was everywhere and her mucky paws were already turning my clean vehicle into a soapy mess. I was pissed. The question was, what to do?
I opened my door, making it clear that if she didn't get off my car it would be the last car she ever cleaned. Really what I said was, "fuck off and get a job".

The light changed to green, and with no one else waiting to turn, I carried on shouting at this wretched soul. Out of the corner of my eye I saw a man approaching, not a large man, but a man large enough to make me think twice about getting out of my car.

"Problem?" he asked, in a very condescending and off-handed manner.

"Why? What's it to you?" I replied.

I was about to get back into the car when he spoke again.

"She's with me, now pay her for cleaning the car and move on" he said.

"Cleaning the car? The car is clean and I cleaned it, not her" I replied.

My gut told me this was about to get nasty and I started to look around for a cop car or cop on a motorbike, just in case I would need help. There were none to be found, which was strange for this part of town because they are normally free flowing and in abundance.

The man in question was blocking my car door and the woman had taken a few steps back. I evaluated the situation again.

"You're her pimp? Right?" I asked.

"Just pay and leave" he said, in a decidedly threatening manner.

"No, fuck you and fuck her!" was what I wanted to say, but instead I asked, "how much?" This seemed the easy and sensible way to a resolution without violence or damage to my car. The light turned green again, and this time there was someone else wanting to turn, someone who looked as apprehensive as I felt, and someone who wasn't getting out of their car to assist.

"$5" he said, and with that, I laughed.

"I have no cash, other than quarters in my car for parking. Let me see what I have. He moved out of the way, and I jumped into the driver's seat, shut the door and before he knew what was happening, I was around the corner and on my way to a parking spot as far away from the two of them as possible.

Walking back to the restaurant I noticed another woman at a different traffic light, sponge and water in hand and ready to pounce on the first car that stopped. "Ah!" I thought, "it's the old pimp routine I'd seen in San Francisco."

When I decided to go homeless for a week, again, my last book Cardboard City describes that adventure in detail, I had stepped upon the traffic light scam by accident. The deal was simple. A pimp had 20 to 30 workers, mainly women, and he rotated them to different traffic lights every two hours during the day. No one suspected these people were being circulated and that they were beholden to only one man. I found out the real situation one afternoon while I was walking around the San Francisco, followed my nose and, hey presto! This was so obviously the same scheme being run in Santa Monica, and my money was on the guy who'd accosted me as the ringleader.

Two blocks further down, and yes, there he was.

It was time to find out the truth. He looked at me, and I looked at him. He was undecided if I was the same person he'd met just a few minutes earlier, and I could tell by the look he was giving me that he either wanted to run or he wanted to fight. He stood alone, and I crossed the road to be on the opposite side from where he remained standing, thinking I would be safer there. He crossed too. I was a few feet from the restaurant, so I felt a little safer that I would have if we'd met in the middle of an empty street block.

"You owe me?" he said.

"Fuck off, I owe you nothing. You need to clean my car and make it the way it was before your woman ruined it" I told him.

"Where's it parked?" he asked.

I laughed and walked into the restaurant. He followed. I turned around and faced him.

"You want lunch?" I asked.

He laughed.

"No."

"Why you following me?"

"You owe me."

"You're a pimp" I reminded him.

People inside the restaurant were watching this conversation unfold and at the mention of the word 'pimp' a few began to take serious notice of what was going on.

"Can I help you sir" asked the approaching waitress. I could tell she sensed there was an issue and although Harry didn't look out of place in this pub type atmosphere, she knew who he was, or I presumed she knew, and took control.

"Are you harassing one of my regulars Harry?" she asked.

"Harry?" Now I knew his name. She continued.

"Yes, Harry is well-known for making life difficult for people who refuse to pay for having their car windshield cleaned. He's nothing but trouble. Right Harry?" she addressed him directly and without fear. Then she continued, "so, get out of my restaurant, leave my clients alone or I will call the cops and have you forcibly removed again."

"Harry? Not a name I would have put with that face and that accent" I said to him, as he began marching back towards the restaurant's front door.

"Oh, the accent is fake" said the waitress, "but his heritage is real"

"Russian?" I asked.

"You have a good ear" the waitress said.

Harry stopped and just before he exited, he said to me, "I will take you up on your offer for lunch"

The waitress looked at me, and I looked at Harry.

"Why not?" I told him.

My friend Gavin hadn't shown up yet, but I knew he wouldn't care and Harry looked like he wanted to talk, and so did I, so, with the sweep of a hand, motioning for Harry to come back in and sit down and with a nod of approval to the waitress, Harry was about to be fed and Harry was about to tell me all there was to know about being a pimp.

It was like a preacher in his pulpit when Harry began. With a coke in one hand and each sip savored like he was drinking the most expensive scotch; Harry began to chat.

"I know what you're thinking" he said.

"You do?"

"Yes, everyone who knows what I do thinks the same way you do."

"And what way is that?" I asked.

"Look, I am very grateful for the food and drink, but honestly, I have no idea why you invited me in here and frankly speaking, I am not who you think I am" Harry said.

"Then who are you?" I asked.

"Just a normal average working person" he replied.

"Yes, but there's nothing normal about you Harry. You take advantage of people who are homeless and people who are druggies and others who are just on their last legs financially," I was about to tear into him, but then I calmed down and mellowed my verbal onslaught, "you're not homeless, I can tell, and you're making a small fortune from pimping out these poor souls for peanuts. They get nothing, you get it all."

"Not true, I need to make a living, and they just help me out."

"So, tell me Harry, I have been homeless and walked the streets of San Francisco, and I've worked with homeless people for years. Tell me how you're helping them out and tell me exactly what it is you do."

Gavin arrived, saw me and Harry at our table and came over to join us, obviously confused by who Harry was and why exactly he was sitting with me eating a sandwich. I introduced them to one another, without letting Gavin know who this man Harry was and why he was sitting with me. Our conversation continued, and as I motioned to Gavin with one slightly evil look, he understood immediately he was to say nothing and just sit and listen. I knew my conversation with Harry would be over in minutes and Gavin got the same impression by that look I'd just given him.

"Harry?" I prodded him gently, because Gavin's arrival had closed off any progress, I believed I was making and Harry had gone all quiet.

"This is your pulpit Harry, your confessional, you can speak freely in front of us. We won't judge."

"Oh yes you will, but who cares. I do what I do because I am who I am."
"And who are you?" I asked.

'I came from Russia, but when I got here, my troubles began. I was only 15, but I just couldn't understand America and my friends were, to say the least, difficult. I got into a lot of bother, even got out in jail, and then, I had this great idea."

"What was that idea?" I'd interrupted him in full flow and he wasn't happy about that.

"Just listen." He barked. "I met this guy in jail who was a homeless bum. He told me about this business where I could round up homeless people, give them sponges and squeegees, then put them at all the traffic lights, and charge them 50% of what they made form cars whose windshields they would clean. Good for them and good for me. What he didn't tell me was, that so many people were already doing this. So, when I began, I found 20 homeless, mainly druggies, rounded them up, got myself a small van and began to rotate them across the city. That's when my problems began. This city is run by mafia, all vying for the same street corners and after I was threatened many ties, beaten up and told to get out of town, my people, my homeless people, all left me and went someplace else, or just hung out at the beach taking handouts from people and getting high all day."

"But you're still doing it. You just tried to clean my car?"

"Yes, after back and forth and many other attempts, I took on the guys who were doing it here in Santa Monica. I got some friends, not nice people, to help me and put together another 'homeless' crew, and we began in earnest, and now I am the king in this city."
"How many people do you have and how do you make it work?" I asked.

'I have 55 people on a good day, and 15 on a bad. I make them work 2 hours at each traffic light, pick them up and rotate them to the next light. It goes on all day, and often they run off with their cash because they think they are smarter than me. But they're not. They will spend the money so quickly, realizing they need to come back to see me, and then it all begins again. They need me more than I need them, I don't have a drug problem, but most of them do!"

"So, you really are a pimp!" I suggested.

"Yes, but a nice one and I am not black!" he joked.

Gavin at least saw the funny side of his humor. I didn't.

"Well, Harry, I am pleased you came to lunch. I learned a lot. Thanks for being so honest." I said, and then continued, "I hope you find a way to make money other than what you're doing right now, but props to you for trying to make a living. My dad always said, it's not how you make a living that counts, it's making a living that's important."

Harry had finished his sandwich and got up to leave.

"I hope I will see you again, but not in your car" he laughed and as quickly as he'd walked in, he walked out of the restaurant, never to be seen again.

Violent Reformers

I went to a restaurant in Venice Beach one lunch time. I had guests visiting from the UK and we'd taken a drive up to see the sites. Having watched a food show on TV a few weeks earlier, they'd showcased a BBQ place which looked amazing, so with an appetite to devour some ribs, we set off in search of this nirvana.

When I moved to the USA in 1991, Venice beach was one of my Sunday haunts. I used to drive to Santa Monica, park the car, walk to Venice and watch the athletes on Muscle Beach, which is located in a small section of Venice Beach, and then walk back. I would then buy a UK Sunday Times newspaper, which, more often than not, had arrived on the early flight into LAX from London, and been distributed to this one particular book store near Santa Monica pier. There was obviously a large UK contingent living in that area, because if I didn't pick up my copy by 4 PM, they would all be gone. In 1991, there were 'beach bum' types, walking up and down PCH, (Pacific Coast Highway), although not too many, begging for money, but none who were that threatening. It seemed all quite palatable, normal and just the So-Cal beachy thing to do! Fast forward to 2022.

Approximately 906 people are said to be homeless in Santa Monica! What a joke, and whoever published that figure as a fact, should be fired from whatever job they applied to do. There are over 66,000 homeless in LA County, of which the majority, or so it seems, live between downtown Los Angeles and the beach. You don't need to be a mathematician to count them. They are everywhere. There are camps set up on every street corner, under every freeway and all along the beach, where, if you were to make my Sunday walk from back in the day, all the way to Venice Beach, you can see clearly that thousands of homeless people line that particular route, and most of them are unpleasant. It's a situation that's so far-flung from 1991, and so out of control, it's sad beyond belief. These people are real. There are no actors and the swarms that find themselves without roofs over their heads, are a sad indictment of the way hundreds of millions of dollars set aside to sort this issue have been squandered. The worst part of all of this is the resentment these homeless people carry and their ability to organize themselves into angry, discontented mobs of unruly and disgusting human beings. Honestly, with all the sympathy on this planet, there are very few of these people I would like to converse with for fear of reprisal and bodily harm. So sad and so unfortunate. This untenable situation has been made all the worse by our government's inability to try to resolve this problem purely with hand-outs. Cash, phones, and other freebies, have just exacerbated the situation, making it more difficult to find a resolution and encouraging more and more people who do not want to be part of any 'normal' community, to join the throngs of genuinely homeless people and homeless people who just enjoy the anarchy and thrill of being off grid in a mutinous in society. I realize what I am stating is possibly controversial, but believe me, I have met lots of street people and I feel qualified enough to give an opinion that in some ways might seem damming, and in other ways, uncompromising and unsympathetic. Trust me when I say, my deepest regret in life is that we, as a human race, should all be guaranteed a roof over our heads, and our inability to provide this to people who live in the richest, most extravagant country on this earth, is disgusting and terribly sad. To have millions roaming our streets with nowhere to go and nothing to do, and nowhere to stay, is ridiculous. The USA, champions of freedom and entrepreneurship, demagogs of wealth, let millions of human beings into our country every year to live the American dream, but yet, we cannot find a solution for those who are already here and living rough without hope or direction?

Anyway, back to the BBQ in Venice, a restaurant which is now unfortunately closed, and no wonder.

Lining up to pay for food is one thing, being harassed by an angry mob while doing so, is another. This particular lunch time, having parked the car in a not so safe strip mall just outside a not so safe Walgreens store, I made my way cautiously towards this BBQ joint I'd seen on the TV show. It was a walk of only 50 yards or so, but it was like walking the gang plank on a boat occupied only by pirates, all ready to push me off.

"Got some change?"

"Please give me money!"

"Nice phone, can I use it?"

"Do you need these shoes?"

Just some of the comments thrown my way as I nudged closer and closer to the food that I could smell but was suddenly being made to feel very guilty to eat. After all, who would want to devour a huge beef rib while watching this circus going on right outside the restaurant, making guilt, the least of my concerns. My safety, yes, really, my safety, was being jeopardized, with each step I took, and I was in two minds if I should turn around or just wing it into the restaurant, eat and then leave, full, and ready to run this gauntlet one more time or just go back to my car and drive off leaving the thought of beef ribs as just that, a thought.

The people I passed as I walked, were angry, smelly, dirty, and very aggressive, all of them wanting a piece of whatever I had and whatever they didn't. I was sickened by the sheer audacity of some of this mob. One guy in particular, an Asian, made a comment that wasn't only threatening, but suggestive of ending my life so he could claim my car keys and wallet. It was time to be aggressive back.

"You want me to be a vegan?" I shouted at this mean looking Asian. He was about 5 ft 2 inches tall, had long dirty black hair, an unwashed face and broken cracked spectacles, obviously not fitted because they hung off what seemed to be, a broken nose.

"You no eat meat, you give to me, you eat no animals" he sneered, as he spat the words back into my face.

"Get out of my way, you're annoying me and all these other decent people who want to go and eat in peace, and honestly, if I wanted to be a vegan, would I seriously be interested in entering a BBQ restaurant. NO!" I shouted and then paused, "you go be a vegan, I will be who I want to be and I don't need you standing in my way."

"You no nice, you vely bad man" he slurred his words and his English/Asian pronunciation of each syllable made it very difficult not to laugh or correct him.

"What is your problem?" I now had my finger pointing directly into his face.

I decided that before he could answer, I would dart into the BBQ joint and order. There was just no point in getting involved and a small crowd of homeless people were now joining this man on the sidewalk, and I sensed they were baying for blood, probably mine!

Unfortunately, and without too much warning, 6 men followed me inside. The manager, a tall heavy-set character, saw what was happening, and got up from his chair behind the counter, pulling a huge meat cleaver from the back of a wall and grasping it in a manner that suggested he was about to kill indiscriminately!

The group stood their ground, seemingly transfixed and unafraid of the managers ability to decapitate one, if not all of them, in one foul swoop. The cleaver swung mercilessly in the air, its shining steel, glistening with the bravado and menace it surely suggested.

Asian guy, with all the courage he could muster, began to speak.

"You!!! Put that down! We come in peace" he told the manager.

"Get out and get out now or one of you will have one less limb than you had when you came inside" the manager replied. I quickly decided this guy was the owner, not the manager.

Asian man looked behind him and after sensing that he and his 6 or so cohorts could take down the owner, no matter what the cost in human life, uttered boldly,

"Come and get us fatty!"

I laughed, the owner laughed, Asian man laughed, but honestly, this was turning out to be no laughing matter.

"Listen up!" I shouted.

"Shut it," said the owner.

"No, listen up" I persisted. "Let me buy all of you lunch" I offered.

There was an earie silence that transcended the restaurant with the clientele who already eating, and those who were waiting in line to order, transfixed to this scene, which resembled something of a standoff from Clint Eastwood spaghetti western. The good guys versus the bad guys, and blood was going to flow, only no one at that point knew whose blood.

Asian man broke the silence.

"You got everlything, we got nothing. Why we want lunch from you? You just give us money"

"Who the fuck do you think you are?" said the cleaver wielding owner.

"We homeless, we poor, we got nothing, you got evelything" Asian man repeated, while his back-up squad nodded in agreement.

"Get out of here now, the Police are on their way, so you got 1 minute before the come and arrest you" he said, as he swooshed his cleaver up and down, like the madman he seemed to be.

"OR!" I shouted out loudly, "you can all calm the fuck down and I will buy you lunch."

They all thought about it, looking at one another for an answer or some common ground in which they could rifle off a retort, but nothing came and no words were uttered. They just nodded their heads in agreement.

"Deal!" I said, "What do you want to eat? I know you, (I was pointing at Asian man), are vegan, but what about the rest of you?"

As I said this, the police arrived, and Asian man, sensing they were about to be evicted, grabbed his opportunity.

'We all want ribs" he said. And just like that, the standoff ended, happy faces returned to the perpetrators, the cleaver was re-situated back into its correct slot on the rack, the manager went back into the kitchen, and food and drink began to appear as if by magic, handed over to some very hungry homeless men, who by now, were salivating at the mouth in anticipation of what could only be described as some of the best BBQ ribs I have ever eaten. The police who'd arrived seemed to understand immediately what was going on, and they got some ribs too. The baying crowd, of now very satisfied homeless reformers, left with their meals, ready and willing to share with other's who were waiting outside. All in all, a very nice and peaceful resolution, which, in the end, had been defused by the promise of food, and the honor amongst thieves that violence was a senseless manner in which to progress and achieve. With full bellies, and a reluctance to reinstate aggravation on my person when I left the BBQ joint, all the guys who'd been recipients of my kindness came up to me and shook my hand, asking God to bless me and thanking me profusely for making their day. Those who were once bandits, had become reformists. The only question that remained was, for how long?

The Sunday Sermon

Every night, and it's relentless, our local news channels are filled with stories about homeless encampments, homeless shelters, homeless charities and homeless solutions. On August 15th 2023, the AP published an article stating there are 582,000 homeless people in America, clarifying that number by stating these are people who actually sleep rough every night. What they omitted to say was there are actually 2.5 million homeless in the USA. Yes, 2.5 million. How do We know this? A vast percentage of the homeless either sleep in shelters or in cars. Now, tell me why we have spent and probably wasted, over 1.5 trillion dollars trying to fix this issue, when all that's happened is, the problem has increased. The number 582,000 is up from 470,000 the previous year, suggesting that the people in power tasked with curing the issue, have no fucking clue what they are doing! And to top that, the Woke brigade have now decided that the term to be used for a homeless man or woman should be 'unhoused"!!! Who the heck came up with that idea? I bet someone paid millions to have it authorized as the correct terminology use to describe our present-day homeless brigade!

My sermon to them and only them, since they're the ones who have their supposed fingers on the pulse and the cash flow, is as follows.

Stop and think about what you have done. The real answer is, you've done very little. Yes, throwing money at some causes you believe to be admirable might work in some instances, but come on, 1.5 trillion dollars to make an issue worse? Where's the thought process? I will tell you where it is. It's in the hands of hundreds of 'do-gooders' who are doing NO good at all.

My sermons were always short and to the point. I wish these politicians had the common sense to also be short and straight to the point. One day perhaps, someone will get this right, but I can guarantee you now, it's not anyone who is currently attempting to fix it and the sooner they all realize what a mess they've made, the sooner we can get it fixed.

Prince William in the UK has made incredible strides with his campaign to end homelessness and one of the things he's preaching is along the lines of my own philosophy. He's suggesting that all charities pull together as one entity and that they stop competing for both money and the kudos of fixing the issue. He's also suggesting the same 'fix' as me, by throwing the ball in the court of people who are not politicians and letting business moguls have their say in how to resolve the crises. If only I was a future king, someone might just listen to me!!

Aggie The Nazi Lover

She sits, comfortably under a tree, knowing she is in full view of anyone who passes her by. Kids and adults, black and white and Asian, but Aggie, doesn't care. Her hair is greyish blonde and matted, her teeth are black as night and the smoke that bellows from within her mouth from excessive tobacco intake. One cigarette would follow another, creating a continuous, disgustingly pungent fog, which enveloped her whole being, and as Aggie was homeless, it astounded me that she could afford to smoke as much as she did, unless she was prone to pilfering her fix, which was always a possibility?

"Would you like this new wheelie case?" I asked her, one sunny morning, as she lay on the sidewalk close to my usual parking space in Laguna Beach. I happened to have an old suitcase, a cabin sized bag, which had never been used which had been sitting in my garage for years gathering dust. I'd made my mind up that instead of this case using up valuable storage space and in the interests of making my life simpler and less cluttered, I would stick the case in my car and offer it to the first deserving person I could find. Aggie, who always walked around Laguna with her old and decrepit wheelie, was an ideal candidate and as I approached, having made my offer from a safe distance, she blew yet another cloud of cigarette smoke into the air and said to me,

"That would be nice, thank you" in a very distinctive German accent.

"German?" I asked her.

"How could you tell?" she replied.

"I'm Scottish, so I know European accents. Which city are you from?"

"That's a secret" she said, as she bowed her head in reverence and became instantly embarrassed.

"No problem. I am Alan, what's your name?"

"Aggie. I thank you for the case, I will use it, but now, I will just sit here and stay quiet."

I got the message and left her in peace.

A couple of days later, she was back in the same spot, lying down flat, sleeping with her head perched on top of the suitcase I'd given her. She was snoring, loudly, entertaining most people who just passed her by not wanting to disturb this freak of nature. Aggie was out cold, either by luck, from exhaustion or from an overdose. My mind told me it was exhaustion, my heart told me otherwise. Aggie was filthy dirty and in need of a makeover and certainly a bath, but I decided this wasn't the time to disturb her from her slumber and I marched on purposefully, hoping to put this sad site of a human being out of my mind, at least temporarily. Returning from my walk, Aggie was awake, and as I came closer, she smiled and shouted out, "Thanks for the case, it makes for a good pillow."

"Aggie" I said, "Wie Geht Es Dir?" which meant how are you in German. She smiled again.

Aggie, if nothing else, was consistent. Her smile was seemingly always there, but her inability to talk deflected from what I believed to be a more than just a mental issue, of a fear of rejection. I persisted.

"So, Aggie, you woke from you nap?" I asked.

"Ya, I vos tired" she replied, with her German/English accent quite distinctive and clear.

"When did you arrive in the USA?" I took a chance with my luck in the hope I might get more information from her.

"Ah yes, another secret" she replied.

"Aggie, how can we be friends if you have so many secrets?" I asked her.

"My secrets are back in Germany, my life here is just empty, without secrets. Maybe also I do not wish to be friends?" she said, authoritively. I had no idea what she meant, but I took that statement as my cue to leave.

"OK Aggie, I will see you tomorrow if you are here?" I told her, as I began to walk away.

"Please don't go" she begged.

"Aggie, if you want to talk, I promise I will not judge. If you have secrets, you can keep them, but I am happy to make time to sit and listen. It's up to you" I told her. She sat and pondered my statement for a minute or so, taking out yet another cigarette and lighting it up while she looked at me in a kind of uncompromising manner. This would obviously become a huge decision for her. Should she talk or should she keep her mouth closed. I waited patiently for her to speak.

"My father was part of the Third Reich. A true Nazi." She blasted with her full voice, loud enough so everyone could hear her. She seemed ashamed enough that when she spoke these words, her head was bowed and turned down towards the ground. It was as if her shame and her admission might spoil any prior trust we'd formed through our previous conversations.

My choice of words would be careful and deliberate.

"That was 70 years ago Aggie, and you were probably only a baby, so your secret can remain my secret, unless your admission upset some of these people who were passing by when you told me" I said, as I pointed to the few faces who, by now, had decided Aggie was just another homeless bum spouting crap which was unworthy of any further recognition.

"I blame my father for my predicament in the USA" she said.

"You mean your state of homelessness?" I asked.

"Yes, it's all his fault."

"And why is that?" I was curious as to why her father's political party affiliations from so long ago had led Aggie to believe she could blame him for her current plight.

"That's a secret!" she said, as she smiled.

Aggie obviously had a sense of humor, so I smiled too and as I did, I could see her facial expression change in an instant from one of concern and mistrust, to one a little calmer and accepting. I knew right there and then that Aggie's story might be a very interesting addition to the one's I'd accumulated over the years from all the homeless people I'd met, so with that in mind, I perched myself on a metal post next to where she sat and I listened intently to what she was about to tell me.

"Eine Fotze, yes, Hitler, he was eine fotze", she began. I had no idea what that meant but rather than ask and interrupt her, I decided to let her continue, hoping that she'd finish her story, and then I could find out what she was referring to. Having said that, the disdain written across her face as she spat out those words, let me to believe that her opinion of Hitler was less than flattering.

She continued.

"It was the end of the war, and I was 3 years old. We had nothing. No money, no home, no food and no hope of ever overcoming the grief that had been a staggering defeat in the war. My father, he told me this when I was older because at 3 years of age, I don't really remember exactly what had happened. We were moving around so often because the whole country was a mess and everyone who'd taken part in the war was truly ashamed to be associated with the Nazi's and Hitler. It was time to hide, and my mother, a fine woman, gave everything she had to leave my father in peace as the experience of that war came back to haunt him daily. Eventually, and not without drama, my father found work in Hamburg, and my mother became pregnant again. My sister arrived when I was 5, but later that year, my mother died of a rare blood disorder, leaving my father with the burden of bringing us up. Of course, he had to work too and could not cope with his double duties, looking after his children and earning a living. One day, without any warning, my father picked me up from school, something he did now and again, and walked me home, but not to my home, to another home. A lady opened the door, smiled and took me in. I never saw my father or my sister again. I had been abandoned, disowned and left in the care of a complete stranger, someone I didn't know and who treated me, at least for the next ten years, like I was a lepper. When I was 16 and old enough to make my own mind up about who I wanted to be and where I wanted to go, I left in the middle of the night one Saturday, taking a bus to Amsterdam and then a boat to England. I didn't need a passport, I just said I was a refugee and most official people looked at me with great pity and let me walk into their country, unattended and obviously illegally. After spending 5 years in London, where I found work, met a man and became settled, we decided to marry. Unfortunately, it didn't last, but he had introduced me to another woman, one of his ex-girlfriends, who had become my friend, and she was moving to Los Angeles. She asked me to come with her, and I agreed. That was about 40 years ago, although I cannot remember the exact details and exact dates, and I cannot figure out in my own mind if I was happy or sad to be visiting the United States, having been brought up to hate everything about America." I interjected. "You never went back to the UK or to Germany?"

"No, I have remained here and after being married and divorced three times, I became homeless about 7 years ago, after losing my job, losing my home and losing my sanity. My last husband was a German and a Nazi lover, and when we met, because of my father's past, we just got on well and became friends then lovers and then I got involved in his politics and also became a secret Nazi. When we were 'found out', he was suddenly a persona non grata in our little community, I was offered no way out other than divorce and we just lost everything we had and he vanished into thin air, just like my father had all those years ago. After searching for him for years, I gave up, found a lawyer and filed for divorce, but unfortunately my mind had by that time, been unable to cope with the rigors of everyday life, and I just retreated gently onto these streets, and I have remained here every day since. "
"Wow, that's an incredible story encompassing many years, all told in a matter of minutes." I told her.

"Well, I wanted to give the brief version because my life is over now and in fact it was over 7 years ago when I started walking these streets, so someone needs to know and it might as well be you" she said.

Another amazing story from another sad homeless person, and another tail of desperation, outlining just how easy it is to end up with nothing and with no one and with no way to return to a life that once seemed normal.

Michael

He was sitting under a stanchion which I think was about 60 feet tall and just one of the many which propped up the Seattle Light rail in the town of SeaTac, Washington. I had arrived on a late flight into SeaTac airport on a Wednesday evening and decided to walk to my hotel, a Hilton, situated about 1.2 miles from the terminal. It was freezing cold and I was starving. The Thai place I passed didn't look that tempting, but the Jack in The Box fast food restaurant did, and as it was past 7 pm, I walked in and ordered the healthiest option I could find on their menu, the chicken teriyaki bowl. Food in hand, steaming hot and ready to be devoured, I headed to the hotel which was just one block from that restaurant, and as I walked down a slight decline towards its main entrance, there sat Michael, alone, cold and with his worldly possessions spread out around him. His back was propped up against that stanchion and his face looking forwards towards a busy road filled with hundreds of cars speeding aimlessly to nowhere in particular. He didn't even blink as I walked past. He didn't give me a single glance and with me all the time trying to ignore him knowing I had steaming hot food in my paper bag and that he had nothing, nothing at all, and that perhaps I should have offered it to him and gone back to buy another bowl of the same. I went to my room, opened up my bag filled with food and had a moment of Jewish guilt. I just could not bring myself to eat anything, and I was stuck in this moment of should I/shouldn't I? "Fuck it" I said to myself, as the steam from my bowl filled my room with a beautiful pungent odor, tantalizing all of my hungry senses and making my stomach jump hoops as the thought of being filled with wonderful teriyaki chicken seemed so enticing.

I put on my coat, and exited the hotel. Within 2 minutes I was standing in front of Michael. He was engrossed in his bible, and it took a second glance and some loud clearing of my throat noise to grab his attention.

"How's it going?" I asked him

He smiled, and I could tell right away he was rather shy and embarrassed to be sitting in this very unfortunate position.

"I walked past you a few minutes ago" I said, "I had some hot food and I wondered if you might like something to eat?"

"No thanks" came his response.

"Are you sure?" I persisted.

"Yes, I am fine" he replied.

"I am Alan, and I am happy to get you something if you want?"

"Alan I am Michael, and honestly, I am fine. I was about to pray and when you came by, I was studying my bible, so I am good for now. Thanks again" he repeated.

"How did you end up here Michael? I was homeless for a week in San Francisco and it was cold there, but not as cold as it is here" I told him.

"Oh" he said, "I am from Laguna, California."

"I live there!" I exclaimed.

"No way" he shouted, and with that, he placed his bible on the ground and we began to converse.

"I've been there about 7 years" I told him.

"I lived there with my parents, and then ended up here because I ignored all their advice and admonished them for trying to control my behavior. I am happy on the streets most of the time, but in Seattle itself, I cannot sleep there because it's so violent and people like me, good people, not on drugs or anything like that, are abused and often beaten by the gangs of unruly homeless addicts that roam around up there. I came to SeaTac for peace and peace is what I get."

"How old are you?" I asked.

"31" he replied.

"When do you think you'll get yourself back to CA and reunite with your parents?"

"Never!" he replied coarsely.

"So, the damage between you guys is irreparable?" I continued, "no chance of a reconciliation to whatever happened between you?"

All the time this conversation was going on, my hunger was increasing and my food was now probably stone cold and smelling out my hotel room, so I decided I had to bring this conversation to an end.

"Michael, I have an idea, how about I get you out of this bitter cold and buy you a hotel room for the night? I am in that hotel," I said, as I pointed towards the Hilton which stood behind us, "I am happy to put you up for a couple of nights so you can at least sleep and rest and make yourself warm"

"Oh, no thanks" he replied, "I am fine here and Jesus will look after me."

The one thing I have learned in all my years chatting to people like Michael was that NO meant NO. I didn't repeat my offer. Instead, I took $100 out of my wallet and said to him,

"Please take this and get yourself a new bible."

And as I passed the money to him, I began walking back to my room to feast on my not too warm teriyaki chicken bowl. That night, at 2 AM, I got up, got dressed and walked back to see if Michael was doing OK. He had vanished, never to be seen by me again.

The Return Of Bob

I hadn't seen Bob in quite some time. In fact, I presumed he'd gone missing, moved away or perhaps passed away. With homeless and transient people, or, as they now state quite clearly on our woke TV channels, the 'unhoused', one never knows what goes through their minds, where they decide to go and for what particular reason they move on. All I know that is if it was me, and thank God it's not, I would spend all my nights on the beach which is situated close to where I currently live and all my days at the top of the hill where my parking lot is, knowing it's a very safe area, there are many wealthy people to ask for handouts and the weather is calm almost 355 days every year. But who am I to judge? These homeless people who surround us, living in cars, trucks, vans, on grass, on sand and in shelters, under bridges, in tunnels, in parking lots, on street corners, they all, every single one of them, have a mind of their own and a direction that seems totally incomprehensible. Bob, wherever he'd vanished to, was just such a person, always on the move, strutting his stuff, albeit slowly and deliberately, between Newport Beach, Laguna Beach and Salt Creek Beach, his three favorite haunts, revealed to me in the several conversations we'd had in the past. Really there was no harm in hoping that one day he'd return, but after about 5 months without a sighting, I had kind of given up hope, which was a shame really, since this book, when I began writing it, was inspired by Bob.

Some other homeless characters had made their way onto my 'patch', but most of them only stayed a few days and in some cases a few hours before deciding to move on. One particular man, Harold, who was by far the scruffiest and smelliest homeless person I had even come across, decided to get into an altercation with a cop one afternoon, the cop, a female, trying hard to move Harold along to another part of town where 'rich' people would not be as intolerable as they were where Harold had decided to park his bottom. The cop, in all fairness to her, was trying hard to reason with Harold, who, for all his sins, wasn't really doing anything other than lie on a patch of grass next to a bus stop and trying to catch some z's. Obviously one or two of our local residents had complained, which had drawn the attention of our local law enforcement and now, this lady was pushing hard for Harold to vacate his patch of grass, without actually threatening him with imprisonment or citation. Honestly though, how do you give any homeless person a citation? They have no address, no ID and no way of paying any fine, so a good talking to, a coaxing conversation, or just a wee push on their nice side, if they have one, is about all any cop can do to remedy a problem that really isn't a problem, unless you find homeless people an eyesore, which, unfortunately, most 'normal' people do. Harold was adamant, he wasn't budging and the cop, in Harlod's own words, could 'go fuck herself and leave him alone to wallow in his own misery. I was standing watching this farce unfold when out of the corner of my eye I spotted another homeless person on the horizon, a homeless person that looked very much like Bob, although from my memory, Bob was a lot larger and scruffier than the man who was now attempting to climb up the gentle slope on PCH towards me. One or two glances in his direction confirmed that indeed Bob had returned, leaving a very happy feeling in my heart knowing he was still alive and kicking. But as he approached the area where Harold and the cop continued their tussle, I realized that Bob had changed and changed in many different ways, all quite honestly, for the better. As you now know, my last conversation or should I say lecture from Bob, was on the merits of good podiatry, and with that in mind, and not knowing if Bob would even remember me, I decided to keep my distance and see what unfolded.

The fact of the matter was, Harold was at that moment, the star of this very unwanted show, and Bob, well Bob seemed to shy back from any involvement, realizing that participation from his side might just get him kicked out of one of his favorite spots. He stayed back, I stayed back, but poor Harold was now being escorted towards the Route 1 bus stop and almost manhandled onto that number 1 bus as it pulled up, off loaded two people and the cop tried with all her might to get Harold onto the vehicle without injuring him or herself. After succeeding on both counts, Harold was whisked away to God only knows where, and Bob, now rather relieved he was safe, watched the cop drive off and made his way to that Osborn bench, his favorite place to sit down and talk to himself!

It was time to go and find out what Bob had been up to. I walked slowly down the trail making haste for my next conversation with Bob the Jew.

"Can you give me some money?" he asked, as I approached, "I am homeless and need food."

"Bob!!" I exclaimed, "I always gave you money and I tried to get you new shoes, do you remember me?"

Bob stared into nowhere in particular and then in his inimitable Boston/New York drawl, began,

"Oh yes, I remember you, you're the guy with the Nikes. You always gave me money too."

"How've you been Bob? Where have you been? I haven't seen you in months"

I have to admit it, Bob looked good! He'd lost weight, smartened himself up, if that's at all possible for a homeless man with no money, and he sported some brand new, for him, fashionable glasses. His face was thinner for sure but he looked healthy, so I joked with him a little.

"Bob, you look like you've been on vacation to a health camp. You've lost weight, and you have smartened up and you look good!"

Bob thought about what I'd just said to him, crossed his legs while he sat and pondered my words and then spoke.

"Well, thank you" he said, "that's very nice of you to say."

"What's your secret?" I asked him.

"Well, I have been keeping busy and eating right" he replied.

That answer blew me away. How can anyone homeless eat right? Now I was curious.

"Eating right? How are you doing that Bob?" I asked him.

"The money people give to me I spend on good food. I decided my body was not working properly, you know how it goes, you have to have a body that works...."

And off Bob went, into one of his lengthy diatribes about the benefits of healthy eating and the wonders of the modern world and all things Bob! He was back, oh yes, Bob had returned and all was well in the world, at least for Bob!

After listening for five minutes, I made my excuses and decided to leave, but Bob being Bob, hadn't finished.

"Can you give me some money?" he asked.

"Bob I would be happy to, just not today. My wallet is not with me, it's in my car and I am in a rush. Maybe next time." I said, as I got up and walked away.

"Don't forget my shoes" he shouted.

That comment stopped me in my tracks. His shoes?? He didn't want the bloody shoes, he also lectured me on podiatry, if you remember, and the last thing

I expected from Bob was a request for shoes. I presumed he'd never remember that conversation, and how wrong was I?

"Bob!" I shouted, now standing about 30 yards away from his bench, "You told me you didn't want the shoes, remember?"

Bob looked into thin air once again and I could tell that the lecture on podiatry was about to begin, so I nipped it in the bud and shouted again,

"Bob, if you really want new shoes let me know next time I see you and we can figure something out!" And with that I left and returned to my car, hopeful that the next time I saw Bob, he'd finally make his mind up about his shoes.

Dead People And God

The unfortunate part of life, is death. The unfortunate part of death are those who are left to rot, without friends or family, just abandoned to arrive at the end of life, alone. All too often when I have been walking around my local streets in the early hours, before day break, I have unfortunately stumbled across lifeless corpses, in fact, over these past three years since Covid began, I have found 5 dead bodies just lying on the sidewalk, or on the beach or golf course, all nameless, all surrounded by the misery that seemed to engulf their final days.

The first time it happened, as I approached the tunnel where the body lay, I was unsure whether the guy was alive or dead. It looked like another homeless person from afar, but as my pace picked up, and then slowed, a cautious approach revealed a young man, surrounded by drug paraphernalia, his body, spread out in a weird and impossibly curious angle, his skin, grey, his eyes closed and his life, gone. It's a scary feeling, (well it was for me), to see anything dead, let alone another human being, and at 4 am in the morning, the last thing you think you're going to find on a walk you make every day at that very same time. This same walk, filled with wildlife, birds just waking to the scent of another dawn, coyotes running past, their bellies full from another night of hunting rabbits, possums darting in and out of holes in the side of hills and then, just at the other end of that tunnel, the tunnel where this body now lay, the beach, where dolphins and whales can always be seen enjoying their freedom in the vastness that is the Pacific Ocean.

911 is the call to make. Yes, after kicking the corpse, the only way to know for certain he was dead, (my psyche would not allow me to touch the corpse with my bare hands), and realizing that life was long gone, 911, that call, the call no one likes to make.

Explaining to the dispatcher what was going on, answering questions, all directed around the current state of the deceased and his description, the exact location of the body, had I touched him, had I seen him alive. Our conversation seemed to last for hours, but in reality, it was moments and then she passed a message through to the local police force and stayed on the line with me until they arrived. Bearing in mind this chap had died on a walking trail and under a tunnel, access to the cops was going to be difficult and knowing that in America the police rarely walked anywhere and were always content to drive up to every crime scene and just park, I knew it would take a few minutes for them to work out how to get their vehicles into the area where I now waited. I had been instructed not to move and not to touch anything and as this dispatch lady kept chatting to me, I felt that my duty was to watch this dead person as if he was my last living relative, until it was confirmed by someone in authority that I had done my duty and could leave.

The cops arrived, 4 of them, one male and one female officer in each car, two cars total. They got out their cars, headed towards me and asked me the same questions the dispatcher had asked. How did I find the body? Had the body been touched? Was there anyone else around at the time I found him? Did I know who he was? Had I seen him before? After four or five minutes and a short discussion between all four officers, I was summoned by one of the female cops and told I could leave. But before I could do so, I had to pass on all of my information for their records, my name, address and phone number, and then finally she confirmed I could leave. I continued to walk and as dawn broke, the reality of what had happened set in, leaving me praying that such an experience never happened again. The local paper ran an article on the death a few days later, and unfortunately the man turned out to be an unidentified homeless person with a bad drug habit. Poor guy overdosed. Such a shame and what a lonely way to die. Can you imagine living your life on the streets with no home, no food, and no one other than homeless people, the majority of which carry some kind of mental or drug related issues and cannot converse with you or befriend you? You have no family, no friends and no hope and the money you manage to panhandle is used for the purchase of drugs, for which you have an insatiable habit that you cannot kick because there is no assistance for that habit when you live on these streets and the next thing you know, you're overdosing in the middle of nowhere with nothing and no one to help you, and then you die? What kind of existence would that be? Yes, some of these people live and die by their decisions, but what if all the assistance programs to help them hadn't been canceled by repetitive government cut backs? What if, instead of blowing billions of dollars on a situation that is only getting worse, homelessness, we change tact and direction and spend some of that money treating and caring for those like the guy I'd found dead in the tunnel that morning?

Government and morons who run it, I felt, were partly responsible for that man's death. Some of you might say, 'don't be stupid, he did it to himself' and of course, you'd be right in that assumption, but really, could his death, just one of thousands of deaths each day, been avoided? Perhaps it could, but now it was too late for him and we would never know.

And then, out of nowhere, it happened again, and this time it was definitely avoidable.

Some of you reading might want to know exactly why I am out walking at 3.30 to 4am every day? Some of you probably don't care. For those who are interested, I find that time of day very therapeutic, very calming and extraordinarily peaceful. In the 60 odd years I have been on this planet, I have always been an early riser, and when I spent 6 months on a kibbutz in Israel in 1975 and then again in '76, the work schedule that we were subjected to made of a 3 am rise and an 11 am finish, something that's stuck with me ever since those days as an aspiring teenager. When I worked out, starting at 14 years of age, I used to run around the streets of Glasgow at 7 pm in the dark and the rain. It always rains in Glasgow! Around 1978 when I moved to London, I changed my routine and began working out at 5 am enabling me to complete my program and head into central London to work. After that, when they opened a huge gym near my home in South London, it opened at 5 and I used to stand in line to be the first one in. You see the pattern forming? Moving to the USA in 1991, I was amazed when I found most gymnasiums opened all night and with that in mind, my early to bed early to rise routine was enforced for life. When Covid hit and all the gyms closed down, I began walking, which is something I have enjoyed doing for over 50 years. I used to walk back and forth to school each day, covering 6 miles total at the age of 10, and then when going to watch Glasgow Rangers play on a Saturday, my friend Howard and I would walk/run to the game and then do the same on the return after the match was done. We thought nothing of walking the 7 or 8 miles each way. Christmas day was something I never celebrated and I would walk 20 miles just to pass the time of day while everyone else was out celebrating the holiday. Yes, Covid did me a favor. I started exploring my local trails, and expanded my walks to the beach and then into areas, which frankly should have been avoided. My mileage went from 4 per morning to 10 and then another 5 in the afternoon. On these walks, meeting homeless people became a regular thing, and as you have read, some of them began to know my name, my routine and my purpose. There were so many other advantages for walking around at those ungodly hours. The natural beauty that is darkness, illuminated by a rising sun or a setting moon can be quite staggering and some of the images of hunting coyotes, fornicating rabbits, swooping owls and washed-up dead sea animals that I have witnessed have been unforgettable. Pictures, shot on my phone, are spread across this book as illustrations, give you a good idea on what it's like to roam around on foot instead of rushing around on 4 wheels.

As homelessness is now spread across our nation, probably every nation, it's always easy to meet people who are unfortunate enough to be found living rough, and early morning walks provide an ideal opportunity to meet them when they are at their most vulnerable. There's also a certain amount of danger involved when coming across a homeless encampment or even just one or two people lying on a grassy verge trying to sleep, and one never knows of course how they will react when I come out of nowhere and disturb their semi-tranquille state, and whether it might lead to a conversation or just confrontation. Touch wood, to this day, I must admit, I have been very fortunate in meeting only decent and grateful 'unhoused' people.

And there I was, marching down a main road, PCH once again, minding my own business and listening to a book about Tiger Woods. And there he was, lying flat out, face down, nose pressed into a concrete bench at a bus stop. It was dark, he was dead, and I was in panic mode.

Have you ever stumbled upon a dead body? An unrelated person just lying fully clothed in the street, stone dead, while the rest of the world just passes then by? The guy I found that morning was the antipathy of such a scenario. He was fully clothed, wearing a baseball jacket, I think it was an LA Dodgers one but I can't be sure, and he was completely flat face down on a concrete bus-stop bench, his nose pressed into that stubbled concrete surface and his semi-bald head facing in the direction from which I was approaching. I shouted, and received no response and at that time, I feared the worse. I was hesitant to touch this guy just in case foul play was at work, and with that in mind, I instinctively got out my phone and yet again, I dialed 911. Same routine, same result. Within minutes, 2 cop cars and one fire engine arrived. Dawn was now breaking and passing cars were slowing down to gawk, as darkness turned to light. The two cops from car 1, went over to the body, the other two came to chat to me.

Car 1's cops approached the body and nudged the corpse. Obviously to no avail. With a gentle glance over to car 2's cops, one of the cops from car 1 made a knife cutting gesture across his own throat, signaling what we had all believe, the guy on the bench was indeed, dead.

The questions began, with one of the cops remembering me from my first dead body experience a few weeks earlier in that tunnel.

"You need to change the time you walk" he said, as he belly-laughed into my face.

"Yep, and you guys need a shift change so I don't become too well-known to you" I retorted.

After all was said and done, they told me I was OK to carry on walking, and as the ambulance arrived along with the coroner's car, I ambled off in the direction of my parked vehicle, just a few steps from where we were all gathered.

One would think that once was bad luck and twice, very bad luck, and that to ever have this happen to me again would just be God's premeditated humor, but there I was, this time in broad daylight, about 3 months later, walking happily down the very same trail where body number 1 had been found, and there she was, surrounded by empty gin bottles, spreadeagled on the trail, dead as a dodo. Who she was, I never found out, because this time I had company and after explaining to the man who had approached the body from the opposite direction, I was walking that this was my 3rd dead body in 5 months, he happily agreed to contact 911 and give his name and number, while I, taking a leaf out of the Police Manual for checking possible dead people, kicked the corps gently in the tummy, just to make sure she was indeed dead. She was. The poor guy who'd met me at the body turned green and then puked on the grass, so upset was he that when the cops arrived and realized how ill he'd become, they called a second ambulance for his personal recovery and attention. I just walked away, dumbfounded. I mean, come on, how is this possible? Three dead people, all homeless, all on the same trail, kind of, all now in the same morgue.

Made me wonder how was it possible that people end up this way, drugged into submission and then death by alcohol and drugs, or, in the case of the dead guy on the bench, perhaps loneliness and starvation? I never knew what happened to that guy, how he'd passed away, so my assumptions were presumptuous. No matter what, walking was now a seriously dangerous hobby for me and one that I was reluctant to ever give up. To this very day, I still leave my home between 3.15 am and 4 am every day, and thank goodness, most days are just as mundane as they should be.

Throwing Money Away

Having seen first-hand how money is wasted on most people's perceptions of cleaning up our homeless issues, with government and charitable organizations fighting for every cent there is to try and beat the problem into submission, I have come to the conclusion that neither know what they are doing and that the problem with our 'unhoused' friends will just get worse as time goes by.

Religion or politics, the two mainstays in this continual fight for dollars that are seemingly available at will, although the 'at will' depends on the state, the city and the politicians in charge. There's a continual fight on all sides, each one claiming they have the 'cure', but yet that cure is missing in action and the issues of homelessness just get worse and worse, and I for one can see no end in sight and only a progression into oblivion.

I was humbled to visit a place in San Clemente, California, which shall remain nameless for various reasons, as a guest, to witness first-hand poverty that is rife in my own area of Orange County California, a fairly affluent county to say the least. This organization, very well-known where I live, supplies food and clothing to those who need it the most, or so they claim. I know there are tens of thousands of people out there who are suffering, and what they do is very admirable, in its own way, or is it? They, along with many other 'food banks' and charitable causes are continual in their onslaught to provide enough poor people with the items they need to survive each day in our 'rat race' climate. Having walked our streets, meeting many who are homeless, I was dumbfounded by the lack of care and attention given to those who live rough on our streets, whereas at this charitable establishment, set in a leafy street in San Clemente, anyone claiming poverty was free to drive up and take basically what they required to survive. I have no problem in anyone or any organization helping these people, my only issue being, most of them drove cars, some even newer than the one I drove, and most of them were clothed and had jewelry hanging around their necks or wrists or on their fingers. The system at this particular place was simple. The warehouse was stocked with all the essentials, mainly donated, from food to toilet paper to tampons to toys to shoes, and all that was required was for the people in need to drive up, state their specific request, fill up their vehicle and drive off. Now, my perception of this system may be a little simplified and perhaps understated and maybe, just maybe, they have control over who and what gets what from who? But from what I witnessed, it didn't seem too difficult for most to just drive in and out and no questions asked. Perhaps, if I am right, and this particular system is utilized across the board at all such establishments, the people who really deserve these hand outs are the ones who are not getting them? Which then leads me to ask the question, if the government are pouring billions into trying to resolve the problem of homelessness nationwide, would it be possible that on a larger scale the money is being wasted by people who are, as I have mentioned before, a bunch of do-gooders doing no good at all? If we wasted multi-billions in Iraq and Afghanistan, billions which were completely mismanaged, isn't it possible the same exact thing is happening here, right on our own doorstep? Of course it is, but with the way this WOKE planet is now, and nowhere on the planet is as woke as California, one has to speculate that the fear of being 'canceled' also brings out the fear of not 'ratting' on those who are partaking in this mismanagement, therefore making our system a never-ending pot in which to piss away billions and then trillions of tax payers dollars. If the homeless figures across the USA had reduced somewhat in the past years, perhaps my argument could be seen as just poppycock, but the figures show clearly a steady increase, so where's the money going and where are the solutions we have been promised to irradicate homelessness or, if nothing else, reduce it considerably? The more people get poor, the more other's get rich. Sad but true, and I speak as one of the more comfortable in society. I dislike bull-shitters, I dislike politicians and I dislike America's need to see a group of both bull-shitters and politicians standing on a stage in front of a camera, spouting nonsensical garbage about how they are making a difference. Go out and talk to Bob the Jew, Aggie, Michael and the likes, and ask them what they think and how they feel, and see what answers you receive. I guarantee you not one of these people, all mentioned in this book, have ever seen a single dollar from any of the billions that have been thrown wastefully at this out of control situation.

Most of them would tell me I know nothing. How many of them have ever been homeless or slept rough for a week? How many have actually sat down and spoken at length with anyone who is homeless? How many know how to run their own bank accounts and financial affairs, let alone the affairs of hundreds of thousands of poor people?

Prove me wrong, get in touch through my web site, alanzoltie.com, I am always available and happy to converse.

Reunions of Sorts

To find someone you've met before when you believed deep down in your heart you would never see or hear from them again, someone you have conversed with, helped and tried to nurture, still walking and sleeping on the streets, even though you believed in your heart that not only would you never meet them again, but that what you did in the slightest way might have assisted in getting them off these streets, is both soul destroying and disheartening.

Some people like to live rough, that's just part of human nature, but the majority of people I have encountered who live 'unhoused' are desperate in many more ways than you or I will ever know or comprehend.

Some want a house, some want food, some want drugs, some want money and some just want a hug, but most just want an end to this life of misery and torment. A life that's soul destroying, a life that's filled with nothing but hardships and possible violence, a life that's incredibly sad. Spending just one week amongst them, hurt. It hurt my soul, my entire being. It's always been that way with me, ever since my mother slammed the door on a Jewish beggar when we lived in Glasgow, telling him there was a place where he could go and get fed, the Jewish Center on Coplaw St. That one moment in time left a lasting impression on my being, an impression that never vanished, and just grew. It grew into a passion, a passion to help and not to judge, a passion to make promises and to never shirk my responsibilities. I am no saint, never have been and never will be, but I am no shirker of what I see as my duty, that everyone, homeless or not, should have the comfort of a roof over their heads. I have seen children sleeping in the back of cars each night, I see the guy showering with a bucket outside his truck every morning, I see some who are too weak to even stand up and of course I see those who are either too drunk or too high to make any sense, but I see them all and I do not differentiate. They are the needy, they are the meek and they need a roof and care.

When Bob the Jew disappeared again, after displaying the new slimmer version of himself, I honestly thought that would be it. I didn't expect to see him again, although I had thought that in the past and been proven wrong. When the Hare Krishna group went off on their own to find whatever it was they were searching for, I never expected for a moment that I would see them again. Same applied to all the people I'd met, even the guy who I bought ribs for at the BBQ place in Venice Beach. But you just never know, and that's why in life, most things come around in full circles and falling out with anyone is, in my opinion, never the best tact to take, even if you feel they have done you harm. What comes around goes around and that has been proven in my own life several times over. Life is for living, and so, when Madge the Catholic came into view one afternoon, in much the same place where I'd met her for the first time, with a huge smile and a tremendous amount of hope, I marched forward to greet her as the long-lost benefactor I had once been, hoping that she would remember me but not too bothered if she didn't.

"Madge!" I shouted at the top of my voice.

"Who the fuck are you?" she replied. As she did so, I could tell from the smile on her face that she knew exactly who I was and that she was delighted to be re-acquainted.

"You want some KFC?" I asked her.

Her smile returned and her willingness to chat to me was there for all to see.

"I never thought I would see you again" I told her.

"Perhaps I was hungry and remembered you and the kindness you showed me, so I came back" she replied.

"Are you doing OK?" I inquired.

"OK?" she began, "how can I be OK? I am still out on these streets, still being abused and neglected by our government and by some other people who take advantage of my vulnerability, and for goodness' sake, how can anyone spend the rest of their life knowing they will never be anywhere but out here?" she said, as she lifted both arms in an upward motion to suggest I was being ridiculous.

"Well, I have nothing to say on any of these matters Madge, so just let me know what you'd like to eat and I'll go and get it for you."

"Can I just have some cash please?" she asked nicely.

I thought about this and felt that in the interests of peace and harmony, I would give her a $20. I pulled out my wallet and she began salivating. "Madge, are you going to buy vodka?" I asked.

She laughed.

"What's so funny?" I said.

"Well of course I am!" she said, with some authority.

"Then I am not giving you the money. I will go and get you food. Take it or leave it?"

"I'll take it." She said, and then continued, "and what do you want in return?"

"I want to know what you did to end up on the streets homeless? I said, "you told me before that it was a long story and that you were mistreated, but you didn't go into detail, and I want to know what it was that made you walk the streets all these years, so I am going to KFC and when I come back, you better start talking." I was adamant, and she knew it, although Madge had vanished before and there was nothing to suggest she wouldn't do it again. I had to hope that perhaps with some food in her belly she might, once again, become talkative, and so, with that in mind, off I went to get her chicken.

When I returned, she was gone. Nowhere in sight.

I waited, she never showed up. So strange how someone who has nothing and who is in need can just vanish into thin air. I walked around and could not find her. I was frustrated and the chicken was getting cold. Not understanding how Madge could have just disappeared, I took one last chance and went back to our meeting place, about 600 yards from where I'd originally looked, and yes, low and behold, there she was, sitting upright, looking towards me, applauding the fact that I had a bucket of her favorite KFC in my right hand and that her hunger was just moments away from being satisfied.

"Where'd you go?" I asked her.

She looked at me as if I was stupid, then looked all around her, and as if to say, 'you idiot, I went nowhere', stuck out her right hand and asked for her meal. I passed it over without arguing and then sat next to her while she demolished her chicken.

"You were going to tell me what happened to you Madge and why you ended up on these streets, but you never did. Don't you think I deserve and explanation?" I told her.

"Why?" she said, as each morsel of meat passed between her hungry lips, washed down with a large Coke, no vodka included.

"Because I am curious and because you are being fed by me and I am interested in your past" I said.

"So you can gloat on my misfortune?" she suggested.

"Why would I do that?" I replied.

"I can see it in your eyes and I'm ashamed of my past, so that's why. If you're not getting me vodka, you're not getting any more information from me. Understood?" She was being stubborn and pedantic, and I wasn't going to try to coax her any longer. I got up to leave.

"Where you going?" she barked.

"I need to leave now Madge and as you're not prepared to talk, there's nothing more to say."

"Just stay a few minutes longer" she pleaded.

'I will as long as you tell me what happened that put you on these streets all these years back?"

"My past has nothing to do with you, so go away and let me enjoy my food. It's best if I never see you again." She said, and at that point I realized I'd crossed a line and that Madge was gone forever. There's always a fine line with people who are homeless, as we already saw with Bob and his shoes, but with Madge I believed I had half a chance to find out what put her in the current situation, but I was wrong. I got up, ignoring the sadness in her eyes, and I left, again, believing that I would never see that woman again.

May 2024

4 am, sharp, Memorial Day. I'd just swiped my parking card, I have a pass which allows me two tickets per day, and after placing the dispensed ticket on my dash I locked the car and headed towards the golf course and trail. At 4 am it's pitch black and other than street lights which illuminate all of our main roads, when I am on the trail, the only illumination comes from the moon, but only when it's out, or the occasional home bordering the golf course that might be lit up by and early riser. No matter what, I rarely, if ever, find or see any other signs of life at that hour of the day, other than animals, like coyotes and rabbits. Crossing over PCH, a 4-lane highway where I park, with my air pods firmly planted inside my ear lobes and my favorite talkSport radio station from the UK playing through the app, I was suddenly distracted by what appeared to be shouting coming from somewhere behind me. My heart skipped a beat with this highly unusual situation as my eyes scanned behind me, to the left and right of me and in front of me, looking for the source of this voice. Although I always feel safe walking alone at this time of day, (some would say night, and that it was madness to even contemplate walking alone at that ungodly hour), when something like this happens, a voice from nowhere, or the sighting of another human being, it's very hard not to panic or at least cautiously assess the situation, just in case, well, just in case that voice or person becomes a threat. With air pods firmly planted in each ear and the radio blaring through its app, distortion of the facts, true reality, can be, pardon the pun, a deafening experience.

I took out one of the air pods. I looked around again, and there he was, standing in a yellow waterproof suit, hood up, wheely bag in one hand and his other hand raised into the air trying to bag my attention. He was shouting something and shouting quite loudly, but because he was about 100 meters down the road from where I was crossing, I couldn't quite make out what he was saying until my air pod came out of my ear and his words suddenly made sense.

"Time!!!" he shouted, "what's the time?"

"What's up!!" I shouted back.

"I need the time" he shouted again. Now that I'd clarified in my own mind what he wanted, my relief was palpable. Initially, because of the way he was dressed and the tell-tale suitcase on wheels he carried, I could tell he was homeless, but one never knows if from a distance it's a friendly homeless person or perhaps a homeless person who could be aggressive. The 100-meter separation never gave any confidence in determining which one suited the personality or voice, and therefore caution is always tantamount to one's safety. This particular gent, although older and plumpish, seemed friendly enough, his bushy beard and overgrown hair, confirming in my mind that the guy was definitely a transient.

"It's 4 am" I shouted back towards where he was standing.

"What time does the bus come?" he inquired.

Most people when asked this question would probably respond, 'well how the fuck would I know?', but because I walked these roads so often, I knew exactly when the bus came, having seen it hundreds of times over the years and having even chatted one or twice to the drivers who sat at the terminus, or starting point, in Dana Point. The bus was the OC 1, which went from Dana Point to Long Beach several times a day, almost always with no one on it. Well, I say no one, but I only saw that bus as it left Dana Point, or stopped at the bus stop opposite my parking lot, which was probably only its second stop, so perhaps my assumption of it always being empty was rather premature.

Not wanting to make this guy feel like he was wasting his time, and realizing that the first bus was more than an hour away, I shouted back down the street.

"About 10 minutes. It'll be here in about 10 minutes."

"Are you sure?" he asked.

I had had enough of this conversation already, and as he was now taking valuable time off my walk with this distraction, I felt I needed to end out chit chat shouting match with a final statement.

"It's a holiday today, so I don't even know if it's running" I shouted.

Big mistake. He began marching towards me and I knew there and then that this brief encounter might end up being a proper conversation.

"What holiday is it?" he asked, as he slowly approached me.

"Memorial Day" I replied.

"Oh, I remember when I used to BBQ on that day" he said, as his whole person and suitcase rolled up right next to me. "I am Seymore" he offered, almost apologetically.

"Seymore, nice to meet you, but what are you doing out here at 4am waiting for a bus?" I asked

"I need to get to Long Beach, there's a lady I met up there a few weeks ago and I want to go back and try to find her."

"Seymore how long have you been homeless?" I asked.

"Too long to remember, and not long enough to forget."

I had to think about that answer, it just didn't make any sense to me, but it obviously did to him.

"I think you might have to wait about another hour for a bus Seymore. Do you have a place to sit and wait other than this concrete bench?" I asked, as I pointed to the bus stop bench in front of us, continuing, "and what's with the yellow waterproof suit? It's quite warm out today." I suggested.

"Well, two things, if I take it off, it'll probably drizzle with rain, and if I pack it in my case here," he pointed, "someone might take it from me and I will have to beg or steal another one. It's my lifesaver because of the inclement May/June weather here by the beach."

I was becoming impatient, and the fact that my walk had been delayed wasn't a positive for my regimented workout schedule. I needed to end this conversation, and as much as I would have like to know more about Seymore, my patience on that particular day was short and my aim to complete my 10-mile hike before 6 am was now in jeopardy.

"Seymore," I began, "it was nice to meet you but I need to go. I hope you make it to Long Beach, fall in love and get married, and if you do, let me know the wedding date and I will marry you for free. I am ordained." Thinking that was the end of our little contretemps, I turned around and began to walk in the opposite direction.

"I too was ordained" he said.

'Oh shit' I thought, here we go again.

Gavin Newsom

I once saw a great bumper sticker on a car which read, "I wish Gavin Newsomthing!"

My own personal feelings on the governor of California can be summed up in one word. Incompetent.

I obviously do not know this man, but I would like to get to know him, if only to find out what makes him as incompetent and as mediocre as his personality would suggest. In all my years of following politics I have never come across anyone who is able to rhyme off percentages, and irrelevances, as competently as Newsom can. I have watched him in live TV debates, on news channels being interviewed, and read articles about him in many newspapers and I don't believe there's another human being on this planet who upsets me more than he does. Again, I don't know him and I apologize in advance to Mr. Newsom, if indeed he's ever going to read this book, but his ability to play the political game and ignore the real issues that California is going through, is mind-boggling, to say the least. I'm sure, when confronted, he's willing and able to talk his way out of any accusations thrown his way, accusations that, again, in my humble opinion, are warranted and justified, especially when it comes to resolving the homeless problem he has helped exacerbate, but Mr. Newsom needs only to look in his own mirror to realize that both he and the cohorts who surround him have done little if anything to improve or eradicate this situation since coming to power many years ago. I recall when I moved to San Jose in 1994, Newsom was then elected to the board of supervisors in San Francisco around 1997, and then from there he climbed up the power ladder, supported every step of the way by his Auntie Nancy, (Pelosi), until reaching the pinnacle of his political career so far, Governor of the State, Top Dog, The Big Cheese. And now, some 5 years into his Governorship, having promised faithfully to bring our homeless crises under control, we now find ourselves drowning under a wave of false promises, a tsunami of 'vagrants' or 'unhoused' roaming our once golden streets, and a debt ceiling that has been broken so many times, even the wisest economic brains on our planet are at a loss as to why his 35 Billion dollar surplus, making California the 5th largest economy on the planet, has transformed itself into a 29 billion dollar deficit, created by an incumbent who has proudly self-declared to be the only savior of our nation, let alone state. The facts of the matter are, this State, is in a state, and the state it's in is being hampered by Newsom's inability to realize the inevitable and that instead of throwing billions at a crises he knows very little about, instead of wasting millions trying to figure out the issue, instead of paying other incompetents tens of thousands to fix the unfixable, all he needs to do is pick up the phone, call me and, although my ideals may not suit his political ambitions, I can assure him that to resolve our homeless issue without spending more billions, I have the simplest of solutions for Mr. Newsom, solutions that will not only cost very little to implement, but solutions that will be effective and long lasting and solutions that could make a serious dent in this problem which we, the people, are sick and tired of living with.

To prove his incompetence and the incompetence of those who surround and advise him, I would like to take you back to November of 2023. President Ji of China had arranged, though God only knows why, to travel to San Francisco to meet with Newsom and his delegation. Rumors swirled that this was Newsom making his play for the White House and a presidential run, hoping that Joe Biden, because of his age and also incompetence, would pull out of his reelection bid, opening the door for Newsom to take his place. In Any event Ji, of China, had decided to come to San Francisco, seemingly on a whim, which obviously scared the crap out of Newsom, who, in a panic, decided he needed to clean the streets of San Francisco immediately, sending all its homeless residents someplace else for a few days to show Ji that San Francisco was as beautiful today as it had been 50 years ago. Total joke!

There are over 30,000 homeless people living on the streets of said city, with the problem being so out of control that virtually every major store in the center of town has closed down due to continual harassment and theft and every street corner is now covered with people who defecate freely, shoot up drugs hourly and harass tourists by the minute, in their plight to survive every second living rough as homeless vagrants. The question was, how to 'clean' these people up and move them before this important dignitary arrived? Newsom was in his element, planting trees on sidewalks, making the local authorities open abandoned buildings to house those they could coax into moving there, and literally cleaning each sidewalk by hand to make the place look pristine. The folly in this process was summed up by several homeless men who were interviewed on local TV, an interview I watched and that you can probably Google. The camera panned in on the planted trees and then to the 3 guys who were standing around outside their flimsy tents. The process of planting the trees on this boulevard had obviously upset their status quo and they were all none too pleased. The dialog went something like this.

Interviewer "So, what do you think of the governor's incentive to plant trees to brighten up your living space?"

Homeless man 1 "I hear the main man from China is coming. When he gone, we gonna tear these trees down and use them as firewood to keep us asses warm"

Get the point? These people are not there to be moved or cleaned up, they are there because they are unwanted and no one in today's government, in any city, knows what to do with them. They can suggest resolutions, pay for improved housing conditions, open more shelters, and feed them continuously. They can clean the streets, move them elsewhere, give them free cell phones and pay them all $600 per month from tax payers money. The problem is, the problem is not going to go away and the problem with that is that they are not the problem! Government is the problem, only government cannot see that they are the problem. It's an out-of-control vicious cycle, consuming billions of hours of brainpower and billions of dollars in wasted funding for programs that do not work.

No, the only way to resolve this homeless crisis is to do the following.

START FROM SCRATCH and FUCK THE GOVERNMENT

Fire everyone who has made the effort to resolve this issue and bring in those who actually know what they are doing. Karen Bass, Mayor of LA, was last week touring a homeless encampment in Hollywood. One might ask, why? Optics, purely optics. When you watch her trying to console these poor souls, each one more desperate than the next to move off the streets of LA and into some kind of housing, it's all smoke and mirrors. Her city has a proven track record of failing to assist in bringing the number of homeless people under control and under her watch and the watch of her predecessor, the issue has become unstainable and so out of control that the numbers are almost double what they were 5 years ago. Why? Because the programs they have spent billions on trying to fix the problem of homelessness do not work! These politicians are so obviously out of touch and barking up the wrong tree when it comes to trying to fix the issue, it's becoming immoral to even think of squandering more of your money and my money on a problem that is just not being handled correctly. As discussed in my previous book, Cardboard City, I personally feel I have a solution to at least bring this pandemic under control, and I would love the opportunity to present my solution to the 'powers that be' in the hope that someone, anyone, will at least listen, take note, understand their own failings and try my ideas out, ideas that will cost considerably less money than those being implemented today. The United States is a mess, and is being overrun by illegal immigration and homelessness, all funded by ordinary everyday tax payer like me and you. Billions are squandered on useless solutions, when it's easy enough to fix the problem with a little bit of foresight and ingenuity, sadly missing from most of the leadership we have voted in to running our cities and country. It's time to wake up and it's time to act, but it's also time for people to understand that those who they voted for are not the right people to make this happen.

Bob Returns

It was wet, May grey they call it. A kind of Scotch mist was falling from the early morning sky and spring was really blossoming into a wonderful pungent odor called Jasmine. My walk was almost complete and my legs were sore and the Osborn bench was about to come into view.

Bob was sitting there, ready and waiting for my arrival, primed and vocal and almost gasping for breath as word after illegible word tumbled from his hungry mouth.

"How's it going Bob?" I asked him as I walked past, determined not to stop and begin any form of conversation. Bob looked unwell, pale and confused and he'd put on weight, which is a hard thing to do when you're homeless and walking around all day. The Boston/New York drawl that I described in earlier chapters, a drawl which spewed relentlessly from Bob's mouth via his imagination and sub-conscience, began in earnest.

"I just don't know when and where to go to today" he spouted.

"Bob, if you don't know that' perhaps it's a good thing if you just hang out here on the Osborn bench?" I suggested, my feet carrying on right past him and hoping that within a matter of seconds I would be out of sight, out of mind.

"Can you get me coffee?" he asked, his yellow sunglasses hanging down to the bottom of his face, clinging on for dear life and the hope of assistance back up to the top of his nose.

I was forced to stop by his question. Of course, I could have just walked on and ignored him, but hey, this was Bob, and without Bob, this book would have never existed. I came to a sudden halt, turned around and mad my way back towards Bob and his bench, knowing that these few feet backwards could spell at least another half-hour of conversation. As I said, it was Bob, and so Bob had a certain priority in my life, even if it was minimal, I felt deep down, I owed Bob something.

"Bob, do you want breakfast too?" I asked. Bearing in mind that Bob was a true stinkpot of a man and bearing in mind I have a very new and clean car, it would have been so much easier just to pack Bob into my vehicle and trapse him off to one of our fabulous local eatery's to consume as much food and coffee as his poor heart desired, but there wasn't a chance in Hell I would allow this man to sit in my car and ruin its newness forever, so my offer to buy him breakfast was predicated on my driving a few miles to Micky D's to pick him something up, returning fully laden with the sustenance Bob so desired.

"Steak dinner!" Bob was back and wandering off in his own inimitable fashion.

"No Bob, breakfast is all I will bring. Do you want that or not?" I was adamant that Bob concentrate on the task at hand.

"I always sit on the Osborn bench" he reiterated.

I was becoming impatient and decided just to walk away, hoping that by doing so, Bob would wake up from his digressions and realize that his free breakfast was about to disappear.

"Abused and neglected" was all he said, and when he said this, I stopped and walked back towards him.

"You told me once that you were abused Bob, when did that happen?" I asked, knowing full well when it has happened but hoping I might get a little more out of Bob if I persisted.

"Newport beach is lovely, and I go there for vacation time" Bob was rambling now, and the broken cell phone he carried was about to enter the fray.

"Bob" I asked, "do you want breakfast or not?" My patience was running thin.

"What should I do when I die?" he asked me.

"Well, let's hope that you're not going to die just yet Bob!" I replied.

"I've been dead for a long time. No one has ever liked me, took care of me, made me feel like a human being and there's really been no point to my life" he said, and while I was staring him straight in his face, I realized immediately, he was right! Seriously, what was the point in Bob's life or in the lives of any of the other 'Bob's' who were out there wandering these streets. Their lives were seriously compromised by the choices they'd made or choices that had been made for them. There's no telling what

Bob or any of the homeless people I'd met over the years could have done had they been given the love and care and perhaps opportunity that you and I had been given. Instead, to us, and don't dare deny it when you read these next words, they are just a bunch of scum and wasters. Yes, you might sit back and pretend you didn't just read that, but it's true. I have met so dozens of people who lead normal lives who believe what I just wrote. Homeless people are a burden to society, homeless people are to be ignored or avoided and certainly never touched or spoken to, and homeless people are just lazy bums who do not want to work of become part of any normal society. While that may be true for some of them, the facts tell a different story. Homelessness is more than a man-made disease, homelessness is created from misfortune and two degrees of separation, meaning that you or I could have been a Bob, or a Madge or a Dan, but for the grace of God. One wrong turn, one missed payment, one ounce of abuse, one little mishap, and bingo! Homelessness is everywhere, even when it's not. Homelessness is never going away, and is only going to get worse unless things change from the very top, from government, and even then, there will still be those radicals who prefer to live this way than any other way. Yes, I have met the meek, the wounded, the infirmed and the crazies, but amongst all those categorized above, there are still some, devious or clever, depending on your own feelings and descriptions, who relish the ideal of living off the grid and remaining uncounted, unconfirmed and incognito. There are some who make a decent living this way and some who do it because they love it, and no matter what we, society, does to try to irradicate the problem, there will always be those who prefer a homeless lifestyle than what we would call a normal lifestyle.

Bob though was correct. His life had been a waste, or so it seemed. With no one to love or care for him, many years of being abused, walking cross country for decades, alone, hungry and dirty, why would his life be anything other than a complete waste? At least some of the homeless people I'd met had had part of a normal life, but Bob was unique in the fact that he'd had nothing normal in his entire existence. Nothing!

"Bob, how about I get you some food? I'll be back in a few minutes so don't go anywhere"

And off I went, leaving behind this man who had become a kind of fixture on my daily walks but yet was completely unknown to me, and probably always would be.

OMG It's the Krishna's

My drive to Micky D's wasn't too far and as the speed limit was a cool 50mph, I figured I could get there and back in 15 minutes. It's a four-lane carriageway at that part of the road and once you arrive in the city of Dana Point where Micky D's is located, traffic lights and careless pedestrians along with moron teens on the E-bikes, slow you down to a crawl. It was just as I entered the city of Dana Point that I spotted them, dozens of them, all in their robes and carrying on as I'd left them the last time we'd met in San Juan Capistrano a few months earlier. I was sure it was the same crew, only their numbers had obviously grown and with about 25 of them dancing around and having a great time. The Hare's were back, and back with gusto! Dancing, singing and generally making the place brighter and happier, although I'm sure some of the locals would beg to disagree. Bob though was my priority, and getting him breakfast and returning in a timely manner was more important than stopping to seek out an update from the Krishna crew. Or was it?

And there he was, leading from the front, I spotted him only because of his bright colored socks, the same ones he'd worn the day we'd met all those months ago, Arkush!

I pulled over quickly, pissing off the drivers who were behind me, but hey, fuck it, I was on a mission, well, two missions. My first mission, to get Bob fed, and my second mission, to find out what Arkush and his crew had been up to. I parked up, illegally, knowing I would only be a few minutes, if not less, and ran over to where their chanting was taking place.

"Hare Hare, Hare Hare, Mr Krishna, Hare Krishna" It just rang out, all along the street, with many people watching and many others just ignoring this peaceful rant.

Trying to catch his eye through the crowd, I motioned to Arkush with a wave of my hand, shouting at the same time, "Arkush, over here!" Arkush, momentarily caught off guard by my loud Scottish voice piercing the Krishna chants, spotted my gesticulation, smiled and ran over to where I was standing. Without waiting to be asked or offered, he hugged me, thanking me again and again for what I did for him and his friends the last time we'd met, and letting me know that they had increased their numbers through word of mouth and incessant belief and chanting.

"Arkush" I said, "I need to run, where can I find you and the rest of your team? I would love to sit down with you and catch up."

"We are always walking between here and San Clemente, and we are feeding from the various places we can get vegetarian food. You will find us, we are not hard to miss" he said, as he smiled and ran back to his chanting brothers.

"Are you still homeless?" I shouted.

Arkush turned back towards me and said, "NO! You saved us."
I had no idea what he meant by that but I had to find out. I ran back to my car, which was creating an obstacle for those trying to get around me, hopped in and headed to McDonalds. Ten minutes later, two large breakfasts in my possession, I was back on the road and ready to feed Bob. All in all, I'd been gone for about 25 minutes, and when I arrived back at the spot where I'd left Bob, he was nowhere to be seen.

"Fuck!" I shouted at the top of my voice, looking around and trying to see if I could spot Bob on the grass or perhaps walking towards the bus stop. Bob loved to ride the Number 1 bus up and down the coast to Long Beach, but as I scanned around, Bob was nowhere in sight.

Two hot breakfasts were about to go to waste, and there was nothing I could do about it. I ran back to the car, jumped behind the wheel and headed up towards the local shopping mall to check if Bob was there. He wasn't. I found a parking spot, and decided to walk back to where I'd originally stopped to chat to Bob, hoping he might be found somewhere in between. He couldn't walk that fast and he was always dragging his wheely case behind him. I figured he must be somewhere close and that in the half hour or so I had been away, his possible walking circle was fairly limited. I was beginning to rue the fact I'd stopped to chat to Arkush, but hey, who knew what Bob was capable of or indeed where he'd disappeared to? It wasn't the first time and it would not be the last.

His drawl was unmistakable, and I could hear it from 400 ft away. He was situated behind a bush, not even a large bush, taking a dump. There were bathrooms not too far away, Bob however chose to defecate with the rabbits and squirrels.

"Bob!" I shouted, "stop being a homeless bum and get your arse out here so we can eat breakfast."
All I could hear after making that accusation was "fuck, shit, fuck, fuck!"
Bob wasn't impressed. He emerged from his place of defecation, cursing and swearing as if his life depended on it. His choice of words matching his foul

mood. It was time to calm him down.

"Bob, it's warm and delicious and I know you love it, so why not come on over here to the bench and eat something before it gets cold."

Bob stumbled out of the bushes while pulling up his pants, all to the amusement of passersby's, most of who were laughing or pointing at Bob and his unfortunate state of undress, before realizing exactly what Bob had just done and then turning away in disgust as the realization of Bob's defecation in the bushes along with the pungent odor of his shit as it punctured they're oh so fragile lungs. What a mess, although the squirrels and flies seemed to be enjoying Bob's ablutions! On the Osborn bench, Bob sat, pensive and I could tell he was about to deliver me one of his famous diatribes, although on what subject, remained to be seen. I opened the bags and spread the food out in front of him and he began to eat slowly, all the time pondering his next words.

"When I was 14," he began, "my life was so bad. I was abused you know."

Bob was repetitious, to say the least.

"Then…" he continued, "then I decided to start walking. My Grandmother had taken me to see a movie about a man who walked across America, but I can't remember his name."

"Forrest, Forrest Gump" I interjected, but Bob didn't care and as he took another mouthful of his breakfast, he just carried on talking.

"Well, if this man could do it, so could I. I was 14, and abused" he said.

"Yes Bob, you told me" I replied.

"So, the next day I walked from my grandmother's home in the Bronx to central Park. That's in New York city, did you know that?" he asked me. Before I could reply, he was talking again.

"I got to the park, and when I arrived, some boys beat me up. I was beaten up and abused again. I don't know why, but I was. Then I went to the hospital, I remember the hospital, it was close to the park. They gave me a bed, but I left, I hated the hospital. I had nothing. They called my grandmother but she didn't care. I was abused you know." He repeated.

"Bob, you were 14?" I asked, and then continued, "but I thought your grandmother abandoned you at an earlier age and you were in the foster care system?"

"I already told you that. Don't you listen? Listening is a good part of being a good person. People who listen are much better people than those who don't." Bob said. And I thought to myself, here we go, another lecture is coming my way. Before I had a chance to think too much, Bob was off again, back into the bushes, but this time to pee. Bob didn't care, but the people who passed us did. One shouted out, 'filthy scumbag" as he passed Bob, who was urinating quite freely amongst the shrubbery at the side of the pathway.

"Give the guy a break!" I shouted back at the passer by. He ignored my plea, sticking his middle finger up at me in a gesture of defiance, and walked on.

"People hate me" said Bob, as he came out of the bushes again.

"Bob, maybe if you used the bathrooms around the corner, people who live and work here would appreciate your sanitary exploits in a much more caring fashion?" Bob stopped, looked at me, was about to say something, presumably sarcastic or rude, thought better of it and then, after giving me a steely eyed glare, sat down and began to chat again.

"My grandmother was nice, then she wasn't, then she was just horrible to me. I was abused you know!"

"Bob, there's a bathroom around that corner" I said, as I pointed, "please try to use it. It's not nice to pee and shit where people walk." I half expected him to tell me to go away and leave him alone, but he took it on the chin and then said, "when I use a bathroom, unless it's a clean one with no one in it, I get abused."

"What do you mean?" I asked him.

"People just abuse me. I am better off out here and I am better off alone. Now, if you have nothing else to say to me, I would like to make a call" he said, as he took out his broken, and innactive cell phone and pretended to dial a number. It looked like my time was up, but I thought I would try one more tact before leaving just to see if Bob would continue his story.

"You calling your grandmother?" I asked him.

"How do you know about my grandmother?" came his response.

"You just told me you left her home at 14 and walked to Central Park, went into hospital and left. What you never told me Bob, is where you went after that and if you ever saw your grandmother again."

"She abused me" he said, and then took his phone, turned his back on me, facing the opposite end of the bench where I was sitting, and began this bogus conversation with God only knows who? It was time for me to leave. I got up and walked away, and Bob? Well Bob was engrossed in his call with no one in particular, but at least he'd been fed and would hopefully live to see another day.

Once a Jew, always a Jew

"Bob, you're just going to sit here all week?" I asked him. It was 24 hours later and after our last conversation, I presumed Bob would have moved on, but I was wrong. He sat there, on his bench, the Osborn bench, playing with his long grey matted beard, his cell phone on his lap and words of wisdom flowing freely from his lips. Bob was in his spot, enjoying the sunshine and not bothering a soul. And here I was, only there to bother Bob. He knew it, I knew it and we both accepted it.

"My mother and father dumped me when I was a baby" Bob began.

"Yep, you told me that Bob, so how did you get from Central Park to here? I asked.

"I am Jewish you know."

"Yes Bob."

My Grandmother took care of me, and I walked to Central Park one afternoon. I never went back. That movie, the one where the guy walked, it inspired me."

"Yes Bob."

"I started to think, that could be me. I thought, what if I walked from the Bronx to California, just like he did. It made sense. No one liked me, and no one loved me, and no one cared if I was there or I wasn't."

"Yes Bob."

He was becoming emotional, or perhaps the memories were just coming out in a different manner, I wasn't sure. In any event, Bob was on a tear and I was there to listen and support him.

"Walking is easy for me. Do you know that shoes really matter and that your feet can be deformed by wearing the wrong ones?"

"Yes Bob."

"Anyway, my feet are perfect, my feet are amazingly supple and my feet took me all the way from Central Park to California."

"Yes Bob."

The fact that Bob was so repetitious and predictable, spoke volumes for his mental state and great unease of being around other people. It was also a red flag for me, deciding what was fact and what was fiction. Whatever Bob was spewing out in our conversation he's repeated word for word several times in the past so it was to no surprise that although my belief was waning, there really was a certain amount of credibility in what Bob was telling me. Or so I thought.

"Where's my breakfast?" he suddenly demanded.

"Where's the rest of my story?" I snapped back.

"I'd love a steak dinner" he said.

"Yes Bob, plain with a baked potato, I know you don't like sauces."

"Yes, that's right, it's the way my grandmother cooked it for me. You know I am Jewish, so I like things plain" Bob repeated for the umpteenth time.

"Bob, how about I go and get you some scrambled eggs and steak from RJ's in Dana Point and bring it back? If I do this, will you promise not to vanish again?"

"Scrambled, not fried" he ordered.

Forty-five minutes later I returned with a takeout box filled to brimming with a plain steak and scrambled eggs and hash browns and Bob, who was yet again chatting on his broken cell phone, became quote excited when he saw me, suggesting to the ghost caller he was chatting with that an important meeting had come up and he needed to disconnect his call in the interest of national security. This made me chuckle and unintentionally I let out a small laugh. Fortunately, Bob didn't catch my faux pas, and after putting his phone back into his pocket, pulling his bushy beard to one side and propping his glasses higher up onto the top of his nose, he sat upright on his bench and awaited the unveiling of his breakfast.

"Bob, please know, the eggs are scrambled and the steak is plain. No baked potato, just hash browns." I told him.

In his Boston/New York drawl, he let out a sigh suggesting he was annoyed and then said to me in a nasally voice, "well they don't have great potatoes in California."

I mean, WTF?? Some of what came out of Bob's mouth was often hilarious and some pure fantasy, but his mental health issues were so evident in every aspect of his character, and I was determined, if possible, to try and place Bob in the right care to ensure not only his well-being but his safety. Whether or not that was even possible was still to be determined.

"So, Bob, what happened after Central Park?" I asked him.

"You see" said Bob, as he began chomping on his steak breakfast, "walking came easy for me. I had no friends, and no family and no pets and all I wanted to do was get away from all the abuse, so walking was ideal. It left me alone to my own self. No one could harm me and no one would talk to me, and for me, that was great. My feet are very nice," he insisted.

"Yes Bob, you told me how wonderful your feet are, several times in fact" I reminded him.

"Well, my day ended back at my grandmothers and I told her that evening she wouldn't see me again. She was happy, but she didn't believe me. I knew she didn't like me and I was a burden to her, in fact, she'd told me that many times, often while she hit me."

"Wait," I paused, "your grandma hit you?"

"Oh yes, every day" and when he said that he began to cry. So, when I told her she wouldn't see me again, she thought I was joking. She asked me where I was going. I told her, like the man in the movie, I was going to walk to California. Then she laughed at me, put her coat on and left the house. That was when I put on my best shoes, took food from her refrigerator, and got all wrapped up in my coat and some extra clothes, giving me more protection, found a carry bag and after filling it with the things I thought I would need, I left."

Bob was well into his breakfast by now but I knew he was never going to finish it while I was around and decided to offer him and out.

"Bob, are you tired of talking, so you need a rest?"

"I walked back to Central Park, and it took me most of the night," he continued, "and when I got there, I was beaten up by a bunch of thugs, horrible people, who took all my food and the clothes in my bag. I was left all alone on the grass, bleeding, I remember crying too. I was only 14."

The thing with Bob that was interesting and so very sad was his inability to comprehend the simplest of tasks and yet, his memory for the past seemed fluent and cognitive. If only it was possible for him to seek professional assistance and for someone to figure out what triggered him and what was true and false. For me, it was just a fleeting glimpse of what seemed, an interesting but sad life. It's a life that I would not have wanted to live, but as most people will tell you, 'There but for the grace of God go I.'

One has to ponder what would have happened had successive governments not canceled all the mental health programs available in the past for people like Bob? Would Bob, and so many others have stood a better chance in life? As a mark of respect to our current administration, both at local and national level, I do not know for sure what's actually available to the Bobs of this world and before I condemn these officials even more, it would be nice to hear from someone who can confirm or deny my accusations that mental health care for homeless people does or does not exist. However, having tried many times to talk to someone, anyone, who knows what they are talking about at the local level, I have unfortunately hit the proverbial brick wall and never seem to get the reply or responses required to confirm or deny any of the above. Why is it when ordinary people are elected as government officials they suddenly forget how to answer their phones or emails, or tell the truth?

"Bob, did you go back to your grandmother after you were beaten up or did you call the police and try to get help?" I asked.

But Bob was already in his own 'dream world', spouting off more crap about military aid to the Congo and how the CIA was going to intervene, waxing lyrical from his podium on top of the Osborn bench. For me, the morning was done without any chance of questioning Bob further so I took my leave and walked back to the car, hopeful that on another day, Bob might just open up a little more. In the meantime, I decided it was time to find out exactly where all these 'supposed' dollars on homeless causes were being spent, and that was going to prove a lot more difficult than I expected.

Show Me The Money

Pathetic. The one word I would use to sum up the way our elected officials at any level, State, local or Federal, have attempted to curtail our national homeless crises. There's nothing out there in the way of a resolution that I would describe as 'workable and sustainable' and there are too many cooks just spoiling the broth, with more and more helpless homeless people looking for someone to make them broth. Even yesterday, and at the time of writing this chapter, the city of Los Angeles announced that they would be providing 'hotel' like accommodation for all of their homeless or 'unhoused' residents, offering them free food, free cell phone, free iPad's, free beds and the freedom to come and go as they wished, with all services, including room service and cleaning, provided by? Guess who? Yep, us, the plain old ordinary law-abiding, tax-paying citizens of the state of California and the city of Los Angeles. There must be someone out there other than me that finds this whole situation just scandalous? Why, and I ask this as a humanitarian not as a greedy bastard who isn't interested in helping out when required, are we squandering more and more money to feed the issue rather than trying to resolve it? If I had no money and the city provided hotel accommodation, all-expenses paid, with room service thrown in, why on earth would I even make an attempt to work or find a job or get myself off the streets? There would be little, if at all, no point. To provide people like Bob with a roof over their head is, as we say in my faith, a mitzvah, (blessing or good deed), but how far can we go on to motivate these homeless people to get out and reacquaint themselves with a normal society without going through the process of spoiling them rotten and treating them like the nuisance they have become. I am using the term nuisance because some of them really are officious, skiving, thieving miserable parasites, intent on living off the system because the system makes it easy. Again, these are my opinions and in no way reflect the amount of sympathy and sadness I have for anyone who is homeless. I have lived as a homeless person myself, (again, read Carboard City), so I know the ins and outs of living with the system and trying to ride that system for as much as is humanly possible. Of course, there are tens of thousands who are genuinely in need of help, but there are just as many who are abusing the system to get what they can, as often as they can, without putting anything back in return. Take Bob, a man you now know from the previous chapters you just read. Bob gets a state pension, Bob gets a cell phone and Bob gets money from the government for living 'rough' and yet Bob is always claiming poverty, which, is perhaps debatable due to Bob's large belly and his penchant for the number 1 bus route taking him to and from his 'resort' locations. Of all the homeless people I have interacted with over the years, Bob is the most fascinating, and my fascination with him stems from his ability to walk 3000 miles across country, survive that journey and find a way, daily, to feed himself and clean himself (Bob is dirty at times and other times he's spotless) and make it into the next day without bothering too many others. Most homeless people I have met are intent on milking their troubled situation to the max, bothering anyone who walks past them and often become very aggressive when 'donations' to their own cause is refused. Perhaps I am being judgmental and overly reactive to situations I have witnessed or lived through, but the difference between our homeless colonies and our governing politicians, is, to say the least, almost identical. They are all after handouts, the politicians are asking you and I for more tax and the homeless are asking both you and I AND the politicians for more money. Going back again to my favorite politician, Gavin Newsom, who, just yesterday, admitted on TV that he's missing 29 billion dollars from the state coffers! Missing?? Where the fuck is it, and if he doesn't know where it is, who does? They 'think', and again, I use the word 'they' loosely here, that it may have been misspent either on the homeless crises or on this stupid bullet train project that was supposed to be built 30 years ago between LA and Frisco, but is still in its 'developmental' stage. Total crap. The money is missing, the politicians are corrupt and stupid and the only ones who suffer are the ordinary people like you and me who are paying for the incompetence that is the state of California. Fuck the government is what I say, fuck'em and fire them before they misplace another 50 billion dollars. In the meantime, California plays host to more than 35% of the total homeless population of the United States of America! Figure that statistic out? Why do they come here, and they come from all over America, these people are not just California residents. They come here because California is throwing money at this issue, throwing it like it's going out of fashion, and trying hard to fix the unfixable. It's unfixable because the people, politicians who are trying to fix it, are the most clueless, self-absorbed, self-important imbeciles every elected. This state, once wealthy, is now broke, and Newsom is solely responsible for breaking it. Spend, spend, spend, without accountability. The best way to run a, once proud economy, into the ground and into ruin. So, I ask you, how do we resolve the homeless problem without bankrupting the state because I am damn sure the people who vote in the state of California will never elect anyone who isn't stupid, as proven so many times over the past 30 years. (BTW I would like to make it clear that I have no political affiliations whatsoever and believe sincerely that all politicians are liars and cheats). No, the way to fix the issue is not to throw more and more cash at the problem, but for the government to take a step back, realize they have been wrong for the years they've been ploughing billions into a never-ending pit, and say to everyone who is 'unhoused' ENOUGH!

We need to try to integrate all of the homeless people back into society. I am not stupid enough nor naïve enough to think every single one of them will be or can be reintegrated, but we need to begin the process to give these people back their own self-esteem, to manage their expectations, to make them worthy and to assist them with their drug and mental health issues, all while taking time and care to ensure they get off the streets and never go back. How do we do this? It's not easy, but, in my humble opinion, an opinion that will not be welcome with the many who are do-gooders, is as follows.

1 Stop counting the homeless. Did you know there are many people who volunteer their time to go around cities and physically count the number of homeless people on their streets? It's a fact. These people are saints. Imagine walking dark streets at night in the middle of winter? That's how they do it, when the homeless are at rest, and that's normally at night. The people charged with counting are sent out in pairs, are willing to intrude on homeless people sleeping in tents or under blankets, are also willing to enter, what I would class as, 'no go areas', where druggies and crazies rule the roost, and yet they prevail. They are fearless and are doing a magnificent job of trying to collate what are supposed 'unhoused' souls.

Here are the negatives. The people they count are not always homeless. Often, from my experience, homelessness can be a temporary state for some people. They can be pissed of teens who want a couple of nights away from mom and dad, a man or woman who have had a fight with a spouse or partner, someone on a bender, either drug or alcohol related, who just happens to find themselves bedding down for a night or two to sleep it off. Therefore, the numbers can never be accurate, just approximate and they do not account for kids sleeping in parking structures or layby's inside mom and dad's cars/trucks, the one's I see quite often getting ready for school by washing in the public restrooms near my home. And there are homeless people who sleep in parks, on beaches, hillsides, bushes, forests, etc, all unaccountable. That's why, when the official stats are published and it says 560,000 homeless in America, I laugh, knowing that figure is neared

2.5 million. If there were only 560,000 homeless, it would be a lot easier and a lot less expensive to resolve the problem. If you check all the different websites with available statistics, the numbers vary from 560,000 to 650,000, these sites, rawhide.org and backpackbed.org, to name but 2, are pulling their numbers from somewhere, the question is, where? And why do they differ so much? On rawhide.org, they claim all sorts of horrible facts, (but are they really factual?), such as 40% of the total homeless population in under 18. Go to their site and read on, this book isn't a condemnation of their research or a congratulatory handshake for getting their facts spot on, because, as I mentioned above, we can never know the exact numbers and they will vary from day to day. This is what is wrong with the USA and the way the crises is being run and resolved. No-one knows the truth. We cannot hide the ruth, but the accuracy is there for all to see. Just walk around any neighborhood in any city and the facts will hit you smack bang in the middle of every begging bowl. Homelessness is rife and it's not under any form of control. Let's all face it, government statistics, charitable statistics and any other form of statistic is total BS. The facts are the facts, and homeless people are everywhere. In the end it doesn't matter if the numbers are 560,000 or 2 million, they money being thrown at this issue is being thrown away, and not used to maximize a resolution.

2 Start understanding the problem. Not everyone wants to be homeless and not everyone wants to be housed. It's important to realize there are homeless people out there who choose to live that way. Nothing that you or I can or cannot or indeed want to do to change the way these people live would make the slightest of difference. They enjoy being 'off' the grid and will be living that way for many years to come. We have to accept that as a fact. These 'wannabe' homeless are more of a nuisance than the ones who are genuinely homeless and they tend to be far more radicalized too. By radicalized, I mean trouble makers. Perhaps that's being too critical and perhaps that's being too generous, but from the people I have met over the years, and there have been many, who really enjoy living on the streets, trouble comes with a capital T. They feel the world owes them more than just a living and shelter and they tend to be more vocal about the rights and wrongs of what our government does and doesn't do for them, always asking for more and more in the way of assistance and benefits and, perhaps unfairly, try to run the homeless camps like a cult, when they are not high or drunk. I met several of these so-called homeless people when I was living in San Francisco as a homeless person for a week, back in the day. At that time, unbeknownst to me, it took more than misfortune to end up on those streets. Choice was also an option and the number of those who had chosen to just drop out of our society and live

rough, astounded me. Again, read Cardboard City for a better perspective. The number one excuse for homelessness is misfortune, either financial, medical or homelife abuse. There really are no other excuses. What pisses me off greatly are the 'pretenders', the homeless who milk their misfortune for all it's worth just to live off the state or other people's generosity. It's a bit like welfare fraud, but worse, if that's possible? Pretenders, taking from the needy, and taking unlawfully. More to the point, you and I, ordinary tax payers are footing their bill, which annoys me greatly. It's very hard to weed out the genuine from the fake because they blend so perfectly on streets that do not or cannot differentiate.

3 Adopt a different attitude to the growing mental health crises sweeping our homeless population. Successive governments have shut down a lot of the programs implemented to help rehabilitate our needy homeless people. Those who are genuinely sick, not physically, but mentally. Having worked in shelters for over 35 years, I have met Vets who are in desperate need of assistance in the mental health department and are given very little, if any. I have met these people regularly for many years and the way they are treated, especially as ex-military, is disgusting. They are all suffering from PTSD and other ailments, war related, that could perhaps be addressed, but now, with all these programs shutting down, are left to their own devices to rot and to suffer. It's pathetic to watch and very sad to comprehend their suffering. These Vets were the lifeblood of our army, and although most are not asking for much other than the care and attention they so badly deserve, we, and I use the term WE very lightly, seem to ignore their plight and plough on regardless, ignoring everything they did for our country and hoping that someone else will take care of this issue, while the rest of the world just jogs along regardless. Some of these guys are disabled, some in wheelchairs and some so confused they just don't know what day of the week it is. Yes, there are places for them to shelter, but there's no place they can go to get 'fixed', if that's the right terminology. They suffer daily and they shouldn't have to. Where are the government funds to assist? Spent needlessly on other schemes that these Vets will never see or be part of. Pathetic! And then there are normal homeless, non-Vets, who suffer from similar issues, and one just has to ponder what would happen to these people if they received the treatments they so needed and the opportunities to be rehabilitated and then reintroduced to society to provide some purpose, just like the rest of us do. Wouldn't it make more sense to try this rather than squander billions of dollars on programs that seem to be failing miserably. Again, government is to blame, no one else, just government. It starts from the top and the person at the top is either incapable or unable to make the correct decisions that affect not only the homeless but the tax payers too.

As I have always said, our government at all levels are a bunch of do-gooders, doing no good at all. Until the day I die, I will always believe that. (apologies too for the repetition of that phrase, but it runs deep with what I believe is actually happening)

4 Account for every cent. Where is all our money going? I want to know. I see on TV every night, articles about the millions and millions being spent on homeless issues, well, where are all those dollars going and why, why if we spend so much are the homeless numbers increasing? Gavin Newsom in California will dispute that fact, but then again, he disputes anything that makes him look like the imbecile he is. I can assure you, if you walk around Venice Beach, Santa Monica, downtown LA, you can see for yourself how many people are living on our streets. Ask any shopkeeper, and or any resident of any area in LA or any other major city in the USA and I promise you they will say the same thing. Homelessness is out of control. So, if money is being spent to reduce the numbers, why are they increasing? Because the money is being used irresponsibly and encourages more people to become homeless and feed off handouts from the state. It's not rocket science! It's time to stop the rot, and it's time to change direction and it's also time to change our leadership. Why do we put up with this nonsense and why do we as voters continually reinstate successive administrations at Federal, State and local levels, who are incompetent and clueless? I talk dozens of people at all levels of life, daily. Everyone I talk to kind of agrees with my narrative, yet, we still have an uncanny knack of screwing things up by reelecting the wrong people to the wrong positions and therefore nothing ever improves. It's a vicious and sad cycle, but one we can all change if we just woke up to the realization, we are all being conned. Accountability should be forefront to everything is government, but as far as accountability in fixing our homeless crises goes, it seemingly does not exist, with the left blaming the right and vice versa and the suffering felt by everyone, of either political persuasion, homeless or not.

5 Idiotic Tyrannical Bureaucrats, that's how I would sum up the morons who run our country and state and at all local levels of government in the USA. Power hungry greedy bastards, liars, and unfortunately there are too many to count with the normal few, a sad minority in a procession of stupidity that never ends. With each decision made, worse than the next, there seems a complete inability to come to a consensus amongst us, the voting public, that whoever we elect, is just more incompetent than their predecessor. Where homelessness is concerned, let's try to figure out what Newsom and his cohorts have done with our money? Yes, it's OUR money, and yes, we have no idea what has become of the taxes we have paid when it comes to homeless programs. One program is as useless as the

next, but the question remains, how do we change this wastage into gain, for all concerned?

Perhaps if we asked for a forensic audit on all the money the state of California has spent in trying to solve homelessness, we would be surprised to learn that all is not what it seems? Or perhaps we wouldn't. I hereby challenge Newsom to call me and discuss with me one on one, without his statistical spouting bullshit jargon, for which he is famous, just where OUR money is and what it's been spent on. Show me proof, in writing and then physically, that OUR money has been spent wisely, and then and only then, will I perhaps give him and his state government the benefit of the doubt that they have spent it on the right programs for the right people with the right amount of understanding that they have completely fucked up. Look at the numbers! I am sick of repeating this, but the numbers do not lie and if the government took their time, talked to people in the know and realized their policies are failing badly, would they indeed change their minds and turn things around? I hear you ask, or maybe you don't care, how would I solve this problem, me Alan Zoltie?

Well, read this.

6 When you meet people like Bob, Dan, Dave and Madge, you have an understanding of what's gone wrong and what's missing from their lives to help them rehabilitate into society. Mayor Karen Bass in LA was filmed walking around a Hollywood homeless encampment two weeks ago, Google it, showing sympathy and offering solace to many who live there on a full-time basis. How nice, a lovely PR exercise! But, what on earth did she do to find out what these people are doing there, why they are there and what brought them there in the first place? From the look of the film, seen on most local TV stations, and the way it was reported, not a lot! Mayor Bass, you need to listen to the grass roots movement of your own constituents, the shop owners picking up feces and needles, homeowners, having to walk past tent after tent of both violent and non-violent unwanted street people. Talk to the kids who pass these homeless souls on a twice daily basis going to and from school, and then talk to the homeless residents themselves, but talk in depth, not just for a TV, PR photo opportunity. Go back and spend a night or two living amongst them, go and chat to the people who suffer their mess, go and find a way to make changes, use your influence to make things different, because, right now, you're not helping and nothing is changing.

To make changes, we need to change things up. We need to stop all this government funding, and stop immediately. We are just pouring good money after bad and it will never end. It's a pit that's not only bottomless, it's disgustingly cavernous. No amount of money can fix this issue, unless it's used sparingly and with great efficiency, something that isn't happening right now. To do that, the first thing I would do is remove all politicians from the process. Hard to do, but that's the only viable way forward. Next, bring in reputable business people to distribute and allocate funding. Bring in a team of psychiatric specialists and doctors to offer advice on a case-by-case basis. Sever all ties with any organization who doesn't comply with the above. In other words, privatize the whole process and keep politics out of it. If we can find a way to do that, then we have half a chance of weeding out those who are genuinely homeless and those who are just frauds and who are sucking the system dry. If we can keep politics at bay, then perhaps we can stop playing to the cameras and start making a real difference to those who matter, the homeless. Until then, and until our government realize they are doing a lousy job, our money will be poured endlessly into this black hole of a mess and this will continue on in perpetuity until the right people at the very top wake up and realize what a mess they have made. I am not saying for one moment that their hearts have not been in the right place, but what I am saying is, they have been clueless and unfortunately naïve in their attempts to bring good governance along with sustainable resolutions to a crisis they so obviously fail to comprehend correctly.

Once any of the above happens, and I don't hold my breath that it ever will, then and only then can we fix the issue by bringing hope and self-esteem back to the hundreds of poor homeless souls who roam our streets today.

End of soap box.

Bob Is Still Alive

For weeks Bob had been incognito, leading me to believe he was never coming back. Although his presence was a loss for me, there would be no point in fretting over my abandonment because, as mentioned many times before, Bob was a law unto himself. I wanted to know the rest of his story, but, as my mother used to say, "I wants get nothing". I got on with my life, my continual early morning and late afternoon walks each day, and other than once or twice, I never gave Bob much thought unless I passed the Osborn bench, at which point I would hope he was doing well and silently say a wee prayer for him and his safe passage to wherever he was and wherever he was going. Bob had, in his own way, become a kindred spirit, and although I would never have much, if anything, in common with the man, his whole being had rubbed off on me in a way I am unable to explain, even to this day. Most people I met on my walks knew of Bob, but they didn't know his name or his story, and for me, the story was the man.

These streets show no mercy, no matter what your beliefs, who your God is and whichever way you face to pray, being homeless is a curse, a curse unbreakable by prayer alone, but over the years, homeless people who'd come into my life, whether they believed in God or not, did not deserve to live on these streets, abandoned, alone and so very few of them unable to escape their plight.

Bob had begun his life, as we all do, with hope, but now, like so many others, his hope had vanished and it had vanished so very long ago. Can you imagine being abused and unwanted from the moment you came out of your mother's womb until the day you die? It seems staggering that so many have to endure such a fate, living for many years as a stain on society and a parasite in the eyes of all who judge you. All walks of life have descended into the chaos that is homelessness and from my own personal experiences working in shelters, chatting with homeless people on the streets and living rough for a week in San Francisco, God has little or no say in who ends up in these filthy gutters. It's a shame that we, as society, fail to rectify the injustices that life can throw at the meek, and it's very sad that corrective actions have to come from an incompetent few who try to run our country. Wouldn't life be wonderful if we all pulled together and helped those who do not have what we have and spread our love and care to the few who remain desolate? We cannot die anywhere other than this earth, well not yet, and until Elon gets us to Mars, we have to live with the facts. We are all stuck on this rock and we should all appreciate that if we shared our planet more instead of fighting with one another, perhaps this place would be more of a eutopia than the pigsty it has so obviously become. Next time you pass a homeless person in the street, don't just walk past them, sit down, or stand next to them and realize, they are all alone, they are distraught, they are mostly hungry and they are in desperate need of human interaction, human touch and human care. We have to stop this crisis, and we have to try and stop it now. In years to come it will only get worse and while some people are making trillions of dollars, perhaps it's time to sit down and realize that you can never spend all that you make and sharing may be a better option. Of course, not all those who are living rough on our streets are worthy of anything other than perhaps our disdain, but the majority who live rough need us and they need us now.

And with that in mind, one sunny afternoon in April of 2023, Bob reappeared once again, full of the joys of spring, all wrapped up in the craziest of conversations he was having with a bunny rabbit, a rabbit who, for some unknown reason had decided to plop itself on the Osborn bench, a bench that of course Bob had claimed as his very own. The conversation was in full swing as I walked towards this mesmerized bunny and Bob, who was adamant the bunny was Richard Nixon, and as that bunny bounced all the way into the bushes, yes, the same bushes where Bob had been caught pooping some months earlier, Bob was shouting at the top of his voice, "Watergate was your downfall, but not mine! Get back in your hole, you rat faced devil."

There wasn't much I could say in response to that and I thought hard about giving Bob a wide berth, just to avoid any conversation, but, out of the blue and unlike any time before, Bob expressed an interest in conversing as he blurted out, "where's my breakfast?" right into my face.

My immediate response was short and sharp, and I regretted it the moment it left my mouth.

"Bob, get your own breakfast" I said and as I said it, I walked right past him. Jewish guilt set in about ten seconds later, and I turned around and decided what I'd said to Bob was wrong, so I changed my mind and asked him, "what would you like?"

With Bob, insults seem to fly past him like they were completely irrelevant comments meant for someone else, and in his Boston/New York drawl, he replied, "usual", and carried on conversing with the fresh air that surrounded him.

I left the scene and headed to my car and down to Micky Ds to collect the 'usual' for Bob, all the time wondering what the heck I was doing? Armed yet again with Bob's sustenance, I arrived back to the Osborn bench, giving Bob his food and asking him something I'd never thought of asking previously.

"Bob, did you ever have a Bar mitzvah?"

Realizing of course that Bob's story to date had so many holes and inconsistencies in it, I didn't expect an honest answer or indeed any answer at all, but Bob surprised me.

"My grandmother made me go to Hebrew school, but I was abused. Did you know I was abused?"

"Yes Bob, you've told me many times, but you haven't told me why or how?"

Bob stared into the middle of our deep blue early morning sky and continued,

"Yes, abused for all my life, at Hebrew school they all laughed at me, they hated me, but I went every week and was all set to be confirmed when I was 13, all ready to stand up and sing in the shul, (Synagogue), but they abused me so I ran away and never showed up."

"Who abused you? The other boys or the Rabbi's?" I asked.

"I ran away and then my grandmother took me to see that man running at the movies."

I was getting nowhere fast, and Bob wasn't even touching his food, which was now probably stone cold. I began to think I would never get the truth out of Bob, also thought to myself, 'did it really matter?', after all, what could I do for him even if I knew his whole life story? The answer was, very little. I'd learnt from a very early age, you can sit and listen, you can offer help, but it's very hard to change everyone's lives for the better. There were always going to be casualties along the way, such was the cruelty of our everyday existence.

Bob spoke again, just as I made my mind up to leave.

"I'm Jewish you know, and I like being Jewish. I think I remember my grandmother telling me that my parents disowned me, and I think I my grandmother told me that I should be proud to be Jewish."

He was rambling, uncontrollably, and poor Bob was now reminiscing, which, from the blank stare he was offering, meant it was time for me to depart. I did so, quietly and without fuss, not knowing if I would ever have the patience to sit with Bob again and to find out how he walked from New York to LA, or even if Bob would show up again while I was out and about walking. The reason for his being, I assumed, was truly inconsequential, and that made me really sad.

John, Without Disciples

4.45 am on Monday June 17 2024. He lay on the ground in a fetal position, his clothes dirty and his hair matted, his whole being silent and still. I approached, phone out, ready to call 911, when he suddenly moved. Then he shook violently while bringing his knees further up towards his chest.

"You OK pal?" I inquired. I'd already snapped an image on my phone, just in case the cops showed up. It was always best to show the body in its original position and because I believed this might the 6th dead person I'd found in the past two years, I was well aware of the dos and don'ts of how to proceed when confronted by the possibility of death. The cops had wisely educated me.

"Yes, I am fine" he said, as he jumped to his feet like a soldier standing to attention.

"You don't look fine. Are you on anything?" I asked.

"No, I am sober, but I need $1."

"For what?"

"A cigar" he said. Then he put his fingers through his matted thick black curly hair and continued. "Can you give me $1?"
Unfortunately on this particular morning I had left my wallet in my car and was carrying only my phone and car key.

"No, I'm sorry, I don't carry money with me at this hour. Are you homeless?" I asked.

"Yes, I blame Disney for my current plight." he said.

He was high, I could tell he was high, and he knew I knew he was high, but he was coming down fast and he and I both knew that we both knew that. His twitching and erratic behavior were sure fire signs that he needed his fix.

"Disney?" I asked, questioning his last comment.

"Yes man, they let me go, now I have no money, no home, no friends and no one to turn to. Can you please give me $1?"

"Honestly, I have no money. What's your name?"
"John"

"Well John, let's go into the gas station shop and I will ask the man in there to give you a cigar. He knows me and I can come back later and pay for it."

"No, no, I went in there. He threw me out"

"Don't worry, I know him, and if you stay outside, I will chat with him and sort it out."

John began to walk away, obviously defeated, knowing he'd lied to me.

"Where are you going John?" I asked him.

"Thanks man, don't worry about me." Was all he said, as he vanished around the corner. I moved on.

Driving back from my walk, about an hour later, I passed the same gas station, and John was lying in the middle of the sidewalk, twisting and turning, his body jerking all over the place, his jeans now halfway down his legs, exposing his butt and genitals, and blood running from his face. The question I asked myself was, do I stop and call 911 or do I drive on and forget about John. Sadly, I drove on. I am unable to help everyone, I thought, but that last image of John is still fresh in my head and although saddened by what I witnessed earlier, I sincerely hope some other good Samaritan helped him out. I will drive back later to check, or maybe I won't. It's so overwhelming. One day you feel like you're a saint and the next, a sinner. This homeless issue has to stop, it really does. People deserve better, but some of them have to learn to help themselves first.

Homelessness Around The World

My travels have taken me to over 100 countries, many of them beautiful and some just very ordinary. One of the things that I always look out for when traveling to large cities are the number of homeless people who roam their streets. Homelessness can be defined in many ways, one of which is created by war of course, often referred to as displacement, but in general homelessness is characterized around the globe by a person living rough on a street without permanent roof over their heads, (tents not included), and without a regular income. A pariah in society. China has some surprising statistics, although with that particular government, one never really knows the truth from the lies. The stat that stands out is that China has the largest homeless populous on the planet, which would make sense if only because it also boasts the largest population of any country. Of it's 1.7 billion people, 2.6 million are supposedly homeless. That's probably an underestimation, and during the last 40 years I have been traveling there, I have been witness to many hundreds of homeless people who live on the streets of Beijing, Shanghai and many other cities I have visited. I remember one instance in particular in Shanghai, several years ago, when I came out of my hotel to drive 3 hours to the west of the city to a place called Hangzhou. My driver collected me, as the city was being drenched by a torrential rain storm quite like anything I had ever seen before. This storm had dropped 17 inches of rain in about 2 hours and everything was flooded. We left the hotel and crept along a main road as we attempted to get to the freeway. I was looking out of the rear side window, when suddenly, out of nowhere, a fully naked woman appeared right in front of my face, jumping out of a gutter as she washed herself with rainwater. She was young, maybe 30 ish and really dirty, but as she washed her body in the drains, she was laughing with joy as if to say, 'yes God, today I shall be clean!' This was a sight to behold and although it only lasted a matter of moments, my car speeding off as the road opened up, it brought home to me that our worldwide pandemic of homeless people had no borders. This lady was only one of tens of millions who were at that moment, all suffering the same fate in different countries and in differing time zones, all joined at the hip by the fact they were living rough on streets no longer paved with anything other than misery.

Hong Kong, now part of China, has a mainly elderly homeless population, and I have never understood why? I have been to Hong Kong more than 100 times over the years and I have never seen anyone who looks under the age of 60 walking those streets as a homeless person. I have always been curious to know why this is, and on one particular trip I asked my friend George, who was born and died in the territory, what he believed to be the reason. His answer was simple. He suggested the older people never came to terms with the modernization of Hong Kong and were stuck in the old ways, laid out by a hundred years of colonialism. After that, he added, 'plus they are just lazy bastards!' Which gave me a laugh and may not be too far from the truth because most of the people who live in that region are industrious, hardworking, respectful people. Not that homeless people cannot be respectful or hardworking, but you get the drift.

In London, homelessness is rife, and having worked with homeless people for years when I actually lived there, I can assure you that the population of that particular category was split pretty evenly between the genuinely homeless and the homeless who were, by choice, radicals. By radicals I mean, wannabe homeless, homeless for the sake of being homeless, and homeless to create an undercurrent of bad behavior when required. People may disagree with me on this point, and again, I am discussing from 1978 to 1991, when I was a resident in London, working weekly in shelters and on the streets giving out clothing and food to the needy, but having the opportunity to visit London more than twice a year every year since then, my gut feeling remains the same. Some just want to live on the streets of London because it suits them and their political beliefs.

In Tel Aviv, I have never seen a homeless person, same applies to most of the cities I have visited in Israel. That's not to say there aren't any at all, I have just never seen them, if indeed they do exist. Same applies to Thailand and Bali, never having seen a homeless person on their streets, it makes me wonder where they all live? South Africa is another matter altogether. With the great divide between the blacks and the whites, the majority of blacks living in abject poverty, homeless people, again, mainly black, are to be found everywhere. In Mexico, with the cartels controlling most cities, homeless people are much more common than they used to be and it always surprises me that they're not used as mules or lookouts by the drug dealers? Cheap labor and stacked with knowledge of their local areas. Maybe they are and I just don't know it? The worst city I have ventured into recently is Toronto. Toronto used to be magnificent. I loved going there. A city of beauty and lovely people. This was in the 80's and 90's. Fast forward to June of 2022. Toronto is now a cesspit of homelessness, druggies and the sexually perverse. During my three-day stay,

I was witness to people shooting up drugs in broad daylight on every corner, homeless people defecating in front of children, the perverse, carrying on like they were shooting a porno in the openness of any downtown district, and finally, the number of 'legal' areas to stand and get high, endless. What a mess.

Traveling used to be fun, and probably still is, but the choice of safe destinations is now limited by so many factors, war, gang violence, drugs, and any combination of the above. Sometimes I think it's better just to stay home, but then, what would be the fun in that?

Oh Bob, Where Art Thou?

Supermarket trolly at the front of a rather strange and comical stride pattern, being pushed by a very loud and tormented Bob, brought a picture of happiness to my very dull and mostly boring Sunday afternoon walk, just a few weeks back, in May of 2024. May grey, as we describe it here at the beach in Orange County, was stubbornly static, with a slight drizzle cascading from the sky on top of me and tormented Bob, and as he approached me from the north of the park area, his supermarket trolly and its wonky wheel on the front left making an irritating squeaky noise, Bob stopped, looked around and yes, out came that famous broken cell phone for yet another conversation with no one in particular.

Having found 5 dead people on my walks over the past few years, 2 were a suicide pact between a mother and son, the other 3 were overdose issue, drugs and alcohol of course, Bob to me was proof that there was life after death. He seemed to have a canny knack of resurfacing, just when I believed he was gone for good. He was a man of 20 lives, and spent his in the only way his mental capacity would allow, chatting with dead people, most of whom I would never know. His loud and outlandish conversations with ex-President Nixon, may he rest in peace, were, in my own mind, legendary. Even though I had only captured snippets throughout my time knowing Bob, his ability to dictate terms to Nixon were fascinating and hilarious. One afternoon when Bob was enjoying his Big Mac and fries, he suddenly stood up in front of me, pulled out that infamous cell phone and began to scold Nixon and then Gerald Ford on how they were misusing the FBI and all it's resources. The funniest thing was, and it made me believe Bob might have been in the government at some point, highly unlikely, but I never found out for sure. The eloquence in which he explained to Nixon the failings of his leadership and the mismanagement of certain situations, which blew my mind as I listened to a one-sided conversation, was stunning. Obviously, Bob had severe mental issues, but he also had a very fertile imagination and a creative side that bordered on pure genius. I always thought Bob could have written fictional books, but that was an impossible task for a man so severely handicapped by the folly of his own mental demise.

The supermarket cart was pushed to one side onto a grassy verge, Bob, taken aback by some bunny rabbit who flew out of nowhere in particular, jumped with surprise, telling whoever it was he was speaking to on his dead cell phone, "hang on a minute, I have some intruder I need to take care of", as he swore at the rabbit and tried to kick it into oblivion with a left foot that hardly moved. This could have been a comedy scene on a TV show, for Bob, it was reality and just another everyday occurrence. I just stood and gasped and pondered my next move. Should I interrupt Bob and have a wee chat with him, or should I stand my ground and just watch?

'Fuck it,' I thought, and so, with hope in my heart, I went for it.

"Bob!" I shouted, "get off the phone and let's chat."

Bob, startled and unsure of what direction my command had actually come from, looked around, spotted me walking towards him, and put his phone away without the slightest 'goodbye' to whoever he believed he was talking to.

"Oh, I remember you" Bob said, as if it was only the second time we'd actually met.

"I would hope so Bob. You and I have met several times and spoken a lot." I reminded him.

Bob thought about that and then pensively shook his head in the affirmative. I continued.

"Bob, we're supposed to be buddies but you keep vanishing up to see your other friends in Newport Beach."

Bob checked his stance, looking down at his two feet as if they were alien to the rest of his body, thought for a second or two and then looked back up at me.

"Did you see that intruder? I tried to battle him, but he got away" Bob said, referring to the rabbit.

"Bob, are you hungry? Want to have a seat and chat?" I asked him.

"I don't need food" Bob began, and I felt a lecture coming. "I am full, and I don't need food. Too much food isn't good for you" he said, and as I rolled my eyes in conjecture, Bob spotted my white handkerchief, which was half in and half out of my shorts pocket.

"Can I use that?" He pointed to the handkerchief.

I took it out, and handed it to him, knowing it was now his by right.

"The last time I saw one of these" he said, as he held the handkerchief high in the air with his left hand, "was when my mother and father dumped me at my grandmother's house when I was 4 and as they drove away, my grandmother took out one of these and waived it in the air and shouted to them, "that's right, just surrender your child and responsibilities to me you fucking morons!" Bob was thinking, "and that was the last time I saw them and the very first time I heard that word" he finished.

"What word is that, Bob?" I asked him, knowing it was probably the F word he was referring to.

"Morons!" he blurted out, "I didn't know what a moron was. I do now! They were morons, fucking morons!"

Well, I thought, this conversation has taken a surprising turn.

"Too much food is bad for you" he repeated. Bob then took the supermarket trolly he'd parked on the grass, swung it around so it faced the direction we were headed in, and began his march towards the Osborn bench. Quiet as a mouse and pensive, I followed.

Bob sat on his bench, his Osborn bench, and Bob looked at me as if I was a complete stranger, and honestly, I was. He stared into nowhere in particular, looked at me again and then began.

"When I was a boy, I was abused, and that has left me homeless for all of my life. Why don't people care about me? Why can't I find someone who will help me? Why did my parents let me go? It doesn't matter now, I showed them, yes, I did. I walked and I walked, just like that man in that movie, and I am still walking." Bob was in full flow and I didn't want to stop him.

"When I left Central Park, it was sunny, and when I left New York, it was snowy. I walked, and I walked and after many more years, I think it was years, I ended up here, wherever this is?" he said. He knew where he was, I knew where he was, but for some reason Bob hesitated when pondering where he was. "I like it here. I take the number 1 bus all the time and I go between here and Long Beach and then I come back. It's free you know." He told me. I said, "so you do know where you are Bob?"

He looked and then offered me an explanation, "maybe I do, but I am never sure, you see it all looks the same and after walking for years, I think it was 15 years, I ended up here, and it's my paradise."

"You walked for 15 years Bob?"

"Oh yes, maybe more, and because I don't have a watch, I cannot tell you what time or what day it is, so to be sure, 15 years is an estimate, but I promised myself that, just like the man in that movie, when I hit the water, I would turn around and walk back the other way. Only problem is, I was too tired when I got here and I also liked the weather, so I just stayed."

"How did you walk here Bob?"

"With my own two feet. It wasn't easy and no one gave me a ride and I stopped many times in many places but I had no idea where I was or where I was going.

I just knew from school that one day I would hit the water and that would be the end. The water is over there" he pointed towards the beach, "so that's how I knew I was where I was supposed to be. The water!" he repeated.

This conversation was as enthralling as it was confusing. How does anyone walk from New York to California and survive, especially someone like Bob? Maybe I wasn't giving him enough credit or perhaps he was telling me untruths? Who knew? No matter what, Bob had me hooked and I was in for the long haul so I could find out what the heck Bob had done in the 15 years it took him to walk here? I mean, you don't just pick up a bag, leave your home and walk 2500 miles without money, a phone, means to survive daily and most importantly, a decent pair of shoes and funds and the where with all to keep yourself dressed for all climactic events, food to fuel each step and places to stay? Or do you?

I was intrigued and as I said before, in for the long haul until Bob revealed all. I wasn't sure if he ever would, but I was prepared to spend my time and energy to sit and listen as long as Bob was prepared to talk.

"You ever had a job, Bob?" I asked him.

And with that question, I began to realize that I had made a critical error and asking Bob if he'd ever been gainfully employed was the beginning of the end of our relationship. Of course, Bob had never had a job, nor would he ever have one. Bob didn't need a job, and Bob was doing quite fine running up and down the coastal highway for free on the number 1 bus, receiving whatever handouts he got from the government and whatever else he could panhandle, which, going on Bob's past performance with me, was probably quite a lot. 'A lot' being put into perspective by the way, certainly not enough to maintain his very inadequate lifestyle.

Bob took offence to my question and immediately withdrew for the final time, making it clear from his blank stare and lack of words that our relationship was over. I could just sense that he didn't wish to discuss anything else of consequence with me, nor would he ever do so. Bob was about to disappear for the final time, and this time I had no doubts he would never come back into my life, even if by chance, we bumped into each other again in the future. To this day, when writing this book, that was the last time I saw Bob and I have no idea where he is or what he's doing or even if he's still alive. Bob, wherever you are, you were the inspiration and motivation I needed to write this book, and I wish you all the best and hope you are doing well. Not that you will ever read the book, but hopefully, as all the proceeds of my homeless books go to homeless charities, I live in hope that perhaps, if you are alive and doing well, one of those charities will have you as a beneficiary from the monies they receive from me. Until then Bob, stay well and keep on walking.

Can You Please Spare Some Change

These words always echo through my whole being, cascading in and out and leaving a terrible feeling of guilt. "Can you please spare some change?" Walking past men, women and sometimes children, hands out, willing and often unable to look you in the face as they beg for money to save their entire existence. Some are genuine, other's ore not. Some make signs telling the truth, some just stand in all their glory, spouting lies. Either way and no matter where you are in the world, the age-old trait of begging, often referred to as panhandling, is rife and it's not going away any time soon. The issue is, we all, well most of us, feel that guilt. As we walk past anyone 'panhandling' or begging, carrying our coffees, teas, lunches and dinners, it's hard to imagine what most of these people standing on street corners with little or nothing are going through when it takes the rest of us a split second to decide to buy a latte or a sandwich with money we had had to earn. When it comes down to it, it's not really our problem that they are suffering and that we are not, but yet, who else should be responsible other than you or I? Therefore, guilt, whether it be Jewish guilt, Catholic Guilt, Christian guilt or any other kind of guilt, such scenes of poverty, desperation and depravation, play mind games with our ability to survive and choose what we want to do with our lives as these poor homeless souls just stand and toil on a street corner, hoping that amongst an endless line of passerby's, someone with a kind heart and a few dollars to spare might stop and take pity and offer them a moment of respite with a donation towards that days meal, or fix or whatever else they've decided to do with the coins presented to them in kind hearted manner.

Putting the shoe on the other foot though, can you imagine what it's like to have to stand all day trying to make money to survive, just by begging and hoping that someone with a conscience takes the time to stop, think and then give? This all happens in the space of a split second, and after that split second has passed, money is either coerced or given at will, or it's not, and that possible benefactor has moved on, guilt in hand, or not, and passed right on by without looking, touching or speaking with the starving soul who remains on that corner waiting patiently for another kind soul with greater guilt than the one who just walked past. How demeaning it must feel, begging, asking endless strangers to assist, knowing that the smell from your dirty, smelly body and old clothes are not an enticement to anyone in their right mind to help you out. Knowing that the way you look and the way they look at you does not encourage anything but disdain and disgust from each possible donor. After all, most of us do have a few pennies we can share. We know it, and they know it, but most of us have no intentions to give to any of these homeless people we see daily. Why? Well, the real question should be, why not? After all, we are put on this planet to assist other people who do not have as much as we have, correct? So, why not help those who are standing nakedly unmasked and desperate, right in front of our faces? Why not give, walk away, feeling good deep down, that no matter how small the 'donation' you just gave was, it helped someone who does not have what you have?

My father used to say, 'it's not how you make a living that counts, it the fact that you are trying to make a living that matters.' Again, I have repeated his words of wisdom several times in this book, but they run so true.

Does it matter that they beg to make a living and you don't? The real answer is, YES, it does.

Our streets are no longer safe, our streets are no longer pretty, our streets are no longer just streets. Our streets have become what they were never supposed to become, a refuge for those who have no place else to go. They have become a cesspit of poverty, a cauldron for violence, an escape route without an exit and an encampment for tens of thousands who have no other place to hide. Walk down any street in any major city in the world and you will probably find someone begging, someone homeless and someone who is happy to give money to both. We have become a society of vicious circles. Some earn, some don't and those who don't or can't are supplied by those who can or will. The can and will brigade, keeping the don't and can't team right where they don't want them, out in front of their face's day in and day out. The situation has become untenable. No one wants homeless vagrants on their streets and homeless people do not want to be on these streets, well, most of them anyway, but where else is there for them to go to? Where else would there be mobile wealth that they could find daily for donation purposes if they didn't congregate on our streets. With that in mind, perhaps, if everyone stopped giving, homeless people would vanish overnight? Not a chance. If you and I stopped giving, the crazy people in government would give even more and lose even more. This never-ending disgusting cycle needs to cease and the only way to make that happen is for things to change, and change quickly and in a manner that makes sense and where those currently involved in trying to clear up our homeless crises are kicked out and replaced by those who are better served to make decisions which might improve the mess the current crew have made. Elected officialdom is the perfect vehicle for failure to blame everyone but the elected official. How and why do we keep voting for imbeciles who never cease to amaze in the manner in which they fail? How do we allow failure to turn into more failure and lastly, how and why do we tolerate the incompetence of those who seek to make things better? We are all to blame, and those at the bottom of the food chain, our homeless population, are the recipients of all of our incompetence and neglect. Yes, we do neglect, it's so obvious, especially when 29 billion dollars go missing Mr. Newsom! Let stop all this BS and begin again.

Take Bob, a perfect example. Give Bob the medical care he so needs, give him some hope for rehabilitation, give him his self-esteem back and give him the opportunity to get on in life and perhaps then, and only then, will we see change and change without overspending or sending good money after bad and a contribution into society by people who, right now, are doing the exact opposite and who are draining our coffers dry.

Can you imagine standing on any street with your arm outstretched asking for 'spare change?' I've done it, and I can tell you, it's not easy. I have an accent, so it made a difference, but ask any homeless person in America how easy it is for them to find another generous soul each day, and often more than just one, and they will tell you, 'It's almost impossible'.

I have been quoted many times, not only in my previous books, but in person too, stating, "do not give cash to homeless people, give food." Cash in hand is an elixir for trouble and fuel for addiction, whereas food, feeds a starving soul and hungry mind. A great percentage of the homeless have drug and addiction issues, which, let's be honest, carried them towards homelessness in the first place. In the United States, it is very easy to continue that addiction, even when homeless, through the generosity of passersby who 'donate' their cash believing it will be spent correctly by its recipients. Unfortunately, this isn't the case and in most instances the opportunity to spend to get their next 'hit' overwhelms any desires they have to eat. It's a vicious cycle and one that cannot be broken without the right professional care which isn't available due to government cuts. Go figure! My advice to anyone willing to give money to homeless people they meet is, DON'T! Offer food, offer to buy them a meal, offer to take them home or to a public bath, offer them anything other than cash. I had the opportunity to meet with a young guy a few months back who was begging me for cash and not food. I had offered to buy him any kind of meal he desired and he turned me down flatly, stating, quite sincerely, that he wasn't hungry. Of course, he wasn't hungry. He was too addicted to whatever substance he was abusing to be hungry. After 10 minutes of listening to his assurances that he wasn't addicted to anything and needed the money to buy a bus ticket to wherever, I casually walked away, letting him know that food was all he was going to get. This, quite obviously, didn't go down too well and the barrage of abuse that followed me as I ambled down the road towards my destination, was vile to say the least. It proved conclusively that if we continue to feed bad habits, all the good we are trying to do will go to waste. This applies to our governments too. Don't feed their habits by opening drug zones all over town where they can come to 'shoot up' using clean needles, put our money into care that will rid them of their habits. I suppose it's easy for me to preach, having never been addicted to anything and having never served in government, but honestly, why assist in the wrong way when you can so easily help in the right way?

I digress, and hope that one day all the programs necessary to ease the mental health issues that plague homeless people and also people who are not homeless, will be reinstated and will make a difference to the growing numbers who are sleeping on our streets.

Picking Up the Pieces

Have you ever watched anyone going through a garbage can looking for scraps? Like a racoon, except they have two legs and nowhere else to go. It's the saddest sight on the planet. A human being, bent over a stinking garbage bin, looking for discarded scraps to feed hunger pains that never subside. And then, on the flip side, we have restaurants advertising, two for one or free meals when you purchase X or Y. With millions starving, it seems to me obscene that with so much food available, and so much wastage, we cannot find a system to distribute everything we throw away or simply discard to those who really need it. According to official statistics, we throw away enough food each day in America to fill the Rose Bowl in Pasadena! That's a stadium which holds over 100,000 people for those who don't know, and it's enormous, to say the least. I realize there are many food programs available for those in need, but to throw away so much, seems frivolous and completely insane. How about we try to change things? Oh wait, I forgot, it's difficult to just give food away to homeless people because of previous issues where law suits have been brought against do-gooders donating leftover food which made people sick and under the threat of massive fines and endless bad publicity, it's easier for them to discard the food than to give it away under the threat of continual legal action. America at its finest and a legal system so broken and in need of repair, with lawyers only interested in fees, it's sad and immoral, on both sides.

When I was walking the streets of San Francisco some 18 years ago while doing all the leg work for my book Cardboard City, it made me sick to my stomach to watch elderly men, and sometimes women, bent over, fishing for scraps, inside garbage cans filled with everything one could imagine. Cigarette butts, used tampons, half-eaten ice cream cones and so much more. Just imagine you are starving, you have no money, no means to survive except instinct and it's not a game show, it's real life. The hunger pains in your stomach refuse to recede and there's nothing to do but watch other people walking in and out of stores busying food and discarding some of it into trash receptacles. You might be outside a restaurant, or more often than not, encamped at the back in an alley, and you are witness to the staff exiting and throwing, what you believe to be good food, into the trash dumpster. Tormented, those hanger pains soon turn to desperation and desire to find whatever is available to quell certain death from starvation. There's not much more any human can do other than try their best to survive and by digging deep, very deep, you are forced to plunder these trash receptacles as a last resort to make it through to the very next day or survival on this planet earth is at an end. So difficult a task and so disgusting this act, yet, so common and incredibly unbelievable to watch and consume without throwing up of giving the person committing this act some relief in the form of money or other assistance. Human nature and its ability to instill a survival mechanism is amazing, but on the opposite side from that instinct are those who just watch and laugh, showing a lack of compassion and remorse to anyone put in such a terrible position, with little or no respect for their plight or circumstance. I remember one night in San Francisco watching an elderly man, homeless of course, crack his head wide open as he fell into a dumpster, only to be pushed further inside by a hungry pack of his 'so called' friends, all vying for the same scraps. Horrible to watch, but all too common on streets that show no mercy.

With so many restaurants advertising buy one get one free or in the case of other restaurants who advertise, 'by dinner tonight and we will give you dinner for tomorrow' why not find a way to advertise that the free food will go to someone who needs it? Easier said than done, and very hard to implement I know, but maybe worth a try at some point? Homeless people are not greedy, unless desperate, and most would welcome the chance to eat one good meal a day, where possible. Most don't want more than that and those who live in cars with their kids, and yes, there are thousands of them, are raising those children on scraps and cheap unhealthy diets, making them prime candidates for poor health and malnutrition. Life isn't easy and we make it more difficult each day by our inabilities to control greed and redistribute waste, our waste, to good causes. There are many food banks who try to do great work and help poor families, but there could be so many more and so much more available if some good management and even more common sense were put in place to purpose the abundance of food we have to the right people at the right time. We need to weed out the genuine from the disingenuous, and then we might see fair and evenly distributed assistance going to those who deserve it most. Again, fuck the government, and put this task in the hands of those who know what they are doing. Something sadly lacking in today's society.

Finally

Yes, finally I have reached the end of my journey with this book. A journey that began really with Covid and my decision to start walking our streets at 4 am every day. My gym closed and I used to go there daily. I, like everyone else, was in need of continual exercise, and so, beginning with 4 or 5 miles per day and then increasing to 10 to 15 miles per day, I began to walk, just like Forrest Gump and like Bob. These walks paved the way to meeting up with Bob, who, as I write this final chapter, I have not seen for many months. The same applies as to some of the other characters I have written about in this book, all MIA. I also need to disclose to you now that most of the names of these characters have been changed to protect their identities, not that anyone in our society really cares about who the homeless people roaming our streets really are. I changed their names because they all deserve the respect that life, at this present moment, fails to give them. They are all real people with real stories, and each one has meant something to me and my growth as a human being, while documenting their plight in writing for the rest of the world to read and digest. Compassion for their cause is something I learned years ago, shortly after my mother slammed the door on the homeless Jewish man who visited our house in Glasgow Scotland, and that compassion has grown into a personal crusade to put an end to all homelessness once and for all. Homeless people are everywhere, everywhere we do not want them to be. To change this, we all have to change, as does the government's way of thinking their current process and policies for eliminating our homeless crises. Where their thoughts lie now are definitely not conducive to curing, what is simply, an out-of-control pandemic. A more sensible and distinct change of direction is required and it needs to happen soon, before this crisis deepens to a point of no return. The precipice has been reached and we are about to fall over the cliff into a black hole of no return. The $64 million question is, "who has the knowledge, the desire and most of all the balls to bring this terrible situation to an end, and bring it to an end without burning through more wasted money, resources and most importantly, TIME???"

We adopt animals, we adopt strangers in foreign countries, we adopt trees, so why not begin a charity to adopt homeless people? If we found a million people willing to adopt just one homeless person each, the crises that we are witnessing may just begin to subside. It certainly would be a start. Imagine taking one homeless person each into our lives, taking them home,(of course it's not that simple and that person cannot be any kind of threat to the adoptee), bathing them, clothing them and then feeding them? Sounds like a very unwelcoming and unwanted thing to do, but the effect that would have on the recipient would be extraordinary in giving them back their self-esteem. Everyone out there wants to be loved, if only a little, and showing love to someone who has no one is one of the greatest gifts we can possibly bestow on another human being. Remembering that all of those homeless people out there are just human beings, even the one's with mental health issues, the ones who are addicted to any kind of substance abuse, the ones who are homeless because of circumstance beyond their control, yes, all of them, human and deserving of the care and consideration, we, as mankind are capable of giving. I have a friend who states quite clearly, and I quote,

"These homeless people need to be touched both physically and by another heart that cares"

She was right. Years and years go by where no one comes close to these street people. Most of them have not been touched for decades, and by touched, I mean even a simple hand shake, something we all take for granted, or a hug, again, something most of us receive every day. Would it be so disgusting to walk into your local town or city, find a homeless person and hug them? Knowing you can chat to any of them at any time is also a blessing, for them, not for you. For you it would be, as they say in Yiddish a 'mitzvah' to take the time and make someone's day, pulling them to one side and learning exactly what brought them into the homeless community and how you, as another human being, can try to help them get released from the purgatory they live in each day. No matter how small, each step would be a blessing in their lives, and in time, with perhaps more love and more care, some of them might find a way to rehabilitation and the beginning of a new life back in society. My thoughts, simplistic and naïve they might be, perhaps effective, they might prove. I'm positive there are many good souls out there already trying out some of the things I have mentioned in this book, and all of them are hopefully doing great work and assisting someone somewhere in getting off the streets, but more people need to join in and become a movement for good and a movement for humanity. We alone cannot offer the facilities and care that a lot of the homeless community require but there are lots of qualified people out there who, if willing to give up some time and energy could make the difference that our government seem incapable of doing.

It's been a task to find the right words to put in this book, a book that with a bit of luck will raise not only the awareness required to bring our homeless issue to an end, but raise funds to help with the issues that those who run charities to help in this crisis, will greatly appreciate and use willingly and correctly when deciding what's important and what isn't.

All the books I have written raise funds for their respective causes, and I would like to make it very clear that I do not make one cent on any of the published books I have written and sold. My task as a human being is to help those who do not have as much as I have, or who are not as fortunate as I am. I am hopeful that one day, in the not-too-distant future, I will be able to write another book about this terrible homeless crisis, that no longer exists.

I am open to meeting anyone from government or homeless charities who would like any advice or suggestions on how to resolve our current homeless problem, because frankly, they seem clueless in their current capacity to resolve the issue themselves. Having lived amongst the homeless community, having talked, fed and donated cash to many hundreds of them over the years, I really do feel qualified and experienced in this matter and am ready and willing to jump in to this cauldron of indignity that has become an unwanted plague in my lifetime.

Sadness is not the right word, but disgust might be. Disgusted that we, as a human race, have let this happen, and will continue to let this happen until we realize, the most important thing in life is that NOTHING is actually that important, and with that in mind, if we all just gave a little, to help a lot, just the importance of being here would be enough to satisfy all of our misgivings.

For Those I've Met

Each one an inspiration, each one a memory, each one, a human being
Spread like butter, across street corners shaped like bread
Clinging on to an existence that would destroy most, dangling by a thread
Often transient, often abused, often seriously misunderstood
They bother, they react, they are the pariahs of our faith
Meeting up, like animals to the slaughter but with no immediate end in sight
Feeding from a trough called good fortune, which unfortunately runs empty
Sent into this terminal spiral, this cesspit of long-term eternity
Thinking daily that this must be Hell and that heaven, for them, does not exist

Brandishing and outward bravado to scare away each possible opponent
Sensing their crimes come only from the fact they were born
With no place to turn and very few places to hide, abandoned to rot
Destiny, confirmed by starvation and unlimited torment
Where mental health problems are only surpassed by substance abuse
Diving into cans filled with yesterday's trash and tomorrow's waste
All too common and all too sad, they feed off our disdain
An angry mob, a crowd which keeps on growing
This is 2024, this is a crime and these are the people I have met

Afterword

What if adopting of a homeless person gave you a guaranteed deduction on your taxes? Would you consider it? Would you drive down to your local homeless hot spot, pick out a person you felt was worthy of your attention, befriend them and take them home, bathe them, feed them and clothe them?

What a thought! It's a normal Sunday afternoon, you're sitting at home enjoying a great breakfast when suddenly this idea creeps into your head. You decide it's definitely worth a shot and, hey, there's a tax deduction in it for you at the end of the year, so why not? You get dressed, pick up the car keys, jump into the front seat behind the wheel and drive into town. Arriving some 25 minutes later, you park and decide to walk to a homeless encampment, leaving your car a safe distance from the vile thought of confronting a homeless person from the front seat of your SUV. Nerves are certainly playing their part because you've rarely, if ever, talked in depth to anyone who is homeless, trying hard to avoid the filth and scum you believe them to be, but not this time, this time you are gung ho and willing to cross that communication barrier and find a new friend, a homeless friend, and a possible tax benefit for your CPA to deduct come April 15.

The question running around inside your head at that point, other than the obvious one, "will I be OK and remain safe?", is "which one of the tens of thousands out there deserves my attention and friendship and how will I know if they are sane or not?"

The answers are simple, you don't know! You never know and the only way you'll ever find out is to try. It's not an easy task. What happens if you're rejected, assaulted, conned, overwhelmed and in the end, take fright and run in the opposite direction without actually choosing someone? On the other hand, what if you find someone, someone who is smelly and dirty but coherent and affable? What would you do then?

Again, it's all about that tax deduction. Or is it?

If you were told that assisting someone in need got you a front row seat on the train to heaven, would that make it easier for you to make a decision and adopt a person in need? No tax deduction, just a guaranteed passage to God and all that he provides in his/her offer of eternal bliss.

Tough choice? Right?

My point it, would it take money or the comfort of knowing your salvation to practice the very simple deed of helping someone not so fortunate as yourself, or can you practice that deed, that Mitzvah, without the promise of eternal bliss, or a tax deduction? It is, in my opinion, a no-brainer. You arrive and find hundreds of possible new friends and with a little guile and patience, you weed out the good from the bad, hoping that you make the right choice and from there, you build a rapport with that person over a period of time and then begin to assert your ability to make their lives more tolerable by offering food, clothes and possibly friendship, something most of them are sadly lacking.

As they say on the TV, 'don't try this at home", and of course, don't expect to go to find your newest friend and bring them back to your place for a bath and a meal before vetting them thoroughly over a period of time. It's the easiest thing in the world to be smitten by sadness and compassion, and again, although most of these people are desperate, there's just no need to jump in with two feet. Take your time, find the right candidate, bring them food now and again and then perhaps expand your giving to encompass some of their other needs. Do not buy them drugs, alcohol or cigarettes. Do not give them money, unless you can see where it's being spent and lastly do not offer them any more hope than you can possibly guarantee. There's nothing worse than a broken promise to these people and a broken promise is a setback which is unfortunately, mentally irreversible. They go through hell each day and the offer of any assistance, then broken, is a dagger through their hearts.

Perhaps if more of us took on the task of befriending someone who is homeless, without the promise of eternal bliss, a clear conscious and or a tax break, just perhaps, the homeless would have friends from all over and hope, even if just a little, that one day their nightmare will end. I implore you to please try it and please let me know your success stories by contacting me through my web site, alanzoltie.com. We all have it in us to be good Samaritans. We don't all need to be saints. Remember, we are here to help those less fortunate than ourselves. Make it happen and make someone's day. It's one of the reasons you were put on this earth and be grateful it's not you that is living as a homeless person in America, or homeless in any other place else, in 2024.

Alan Zoltie

Bob-The Jew

Epilogue

It's July 25th, 2024, and this book has been passed to my publishing company for formatting. The book itself is due to be launched in late August or early September of this year, but as I await the formatted version for perusal and a final edit check, I was moved to write this epilogue chapter by an article I just saw on the 5 pm news today. About 4 weeks ago, the Supreme court of the United States, by a majority of 6-3, ruled in favor of eliminating homeless encampments across all states. Of course, this ruling came as no surprise and was anticipated by many who work tirelessly to rid our streets of the chaos these encampments reek across our country. It began in Grants Pass, Oregon, where 1 shelter with 135 beds, services hundreds of homeless people who live in that city, leaving those who could never find a bed, no option other than to set up encampments around the city, creating issues for all of the residents of Grants Pass, who, quite rightly, took umbrage and decided to make haste for the courts and to try an clean up the streets they were living on from all the mess and chaos these encampments left each day, a mess that was seemingly never-ending. After many months going through many courts, the case ended up in front of the Supreme court in June of 2024, and, as I already mentioned, they won and the ruling from that court made it official, no more homeless encampments on public property anywhere in any of the 50 states in the USA.

July 25th, today, one month after that ruling, and our esteemed governor of California passed an executive order confirming the supreme court ruling and making it a crime to set up encampments on public property anywhere in California. Well done Governor Newsom, your incomitance is now complete, and there for all to see. What on earth do you think those who you are now going to displace are going to do with themselves? Where do you believe they will be able to rest each night if there are not enough shelters for them to move into? The facts are there for all to see. There are tens of thousands of homeless people in the LA area alone, never mind the rest of the state, and there are very few beds available to help them. It's a disgusting fact, again, go back to when Newsom decided to clean up San Francisco for the visit of President Ji of China, that we have allowed this crises to escalate to the point where the numbers of people living rough, and as of today's order by Newsom, illegally, that our Governor believes that his course of action, making it impossible for any of these poor souls to rest at night or even during the day, will help resolve this pandemic. He swept away the homeless in San Francisco for a week, planted trees and cleaned the streets, and one week later, after Ji left, they all came back. Tell me Governor, how will you police 50,000 plus homeless people who, as of today, will be living illegally on all your California streets? Who will write them citations and who will ensure they come to court and actually sit in front of a judge? Again, I have said it many times in this book, this is government at its worse, and don't get me wrong, although I have been 'Newsom bashing' for many pages in this book, the issue is larger than Newsom and his cronies, it's an issue the Supreme court has created without making each state take responsibility for creating programs, shelters and solutions for dispersing this homeless crises from public places before confirming them as criminals, which is what this ruling has created. 2 million felons across America and rising, all because we don't know how to resolve a problem which was created by the people for the people, those unfortunate people who will now be chasing their tails looking for a place to stay, a place which really doesn't exist, and therefore making them criminals until our government puts their house in order and remembers, unfortunately too late, that the horse came before the cart and not visa-versa.

Enough said, drop the mic!

I hope you enjoyed the book. Now go out and help someone less fortunate than yourself.

www.ingramcontent.com/pod-product-compliance
Lightning Source LLC
Chambersburg PA
CBHW061735070526
44585CB00024B/2687